California State University, Bakersfield

Runner Life 2011-2012: The RUSH-A Handbook

Dr. Brett Schmoll, Departments of English and History

Matthew Woodman, Department of English

Table of Contents

Notes from Your CSUB 101 Course

Your CSUB 101 Instructor's Name and Contact Information

Name:

E-mail:

Office:

Contact Information for Three Students in Your CSUB 101 Course

Name:	Name:	Name:
E-mail:	E-mail:	E-mail:

CSU Bakersfield

Office of the President

Mail Stop: 33 BDC
9001 Stockdale Highway
Bakersfield, California 93311-1022

(661) 654-2241
(661) 654-3188 FAX
www.csub.edu

July 2011

Dear Student:

It is a genuine pleasure for me to welcome you to "your" University–the exceptional, student-centered learning community of students, faculty and staff at CSU Bakersfield.

As a participant in our First Year Experience Program, you will have a unique opportunity to begin your University experience by enrolling in CSUB 101 (freshmen) or CSUB 301 (transfers). These small classes will allow you to explore a range of specific topics which are all integrated through use of a common reader – "The Other Wes Moore" by Wes Moore. In addition to being the Runner reader for 2011 "The Other Wes Moore" will also be the "One Book, One Bakersfield, One Kern" selection for 2011. CSUB 101 and 301 will give you a small cohort of classmates with whom you can establish early and lasting relationships as, together, you experience life in higher education.

Your University experience will change your life. It will be transformative both intellectually and in terms of your personal development. It will call on you to explore multiple world views and to understand the bases on which other people have developed different values and beliefs, even as you choose to retain your own. As your academic program takes you through our general education requirements and your major, you will also have opportunities to develop your leadership skills, gain a greater awareness of the many forms of diversity and increase your exposure to global issues. As you move toward graduation, you will be better positioned to take advantage of future opportunities, improve the quality of life for you and your family, and contribute to your community and our broader society.

This is an exciting time in your life and it is an exciting time to be at CSU Bakersfield. We are delighted you have joined us for your educational journey to success.

Sincerely,

Horace Mitchell
President

Mission

California State University, Bakersfield is a comprehensive public university committed to offering excellent undergraduate and graduate programs that advance the intellectual and personal development of its students. An emphasis on student learning is enhanced by a commitment to scholarship, diversity, service, global awareness, and life-long learning. The University collaborates with partners in the community to increase the region's overall educational attainment, enhance its quality of life, and support its economic development.

Vision

By 2014-15, CSU Bakersfield will be the leading campus in the CSU system in terms of faculty and academic excellence and diversity, quality of the student experience, and community engagement. Realization of our vision will be advanced by recruitment, development and promotion of excellent and diverse staff within an organizational culture committed to excellence in all areas.

Core Values

In order to honor our purpose and commitment to achieving our vision of excellence in all areas, we are guided by a set of core values that shapes our work with students, with each other, and with the region we serve. These core values include the following commitments:

—Developing the intellectual and personal potential of every student.

—Supporting the intellectual and professional development of all faculty and staff.

—Nurturing a civil and collegial campus environment that values the diversity of persons and ideas.

—Engaging one another with respect, trustworthiness, ethical behavior, and self-reflection.

—Promoting active and informed engagement of faculty, staff, students, and community stakeholders in shared governance.

—Being accountable to the public, alumni, students, and one another for achieving the mission, vision, and goals of the university.

Office of the Academic Senate

Vandana Kohli, Chair
DDH AA209

On behalf of the faculty at CSUB, I welcome all of you to our community. CSUB's central mission is to provide all students multiple occasions for achieving personal and intellectual excellence in the areas of: "scholarship, diversity, service, global awareness and life-long learning." For the next several years, you will have the enviable opportunity to work closely with some of the most dedicated, student centered, energetic, and talented faculty in the CSU system. Under their guidance and tutelage you will learn how to master complex intellectual concepts and ideas, develop valuable, marketable skills, and accomplish goals that will serve you through an entire life span. Your journey will be filled with high and low moments and we will be there to celebrate your achievements and provide support during trying times.

The curriculum at CSUB will challenge you intellectually; yet, there will be times, when you may wonder, "why do I have to take this course – it's not my major?" In those moments, I hope you will remember that our mission is to train students holistically and it may help you if you note and remember what we have designed as learning goals for your cohort. Simply put we expect that all students who graduate from CSUB will be able to demonstrate critical reasoning and problem solving skills. By this I mean that you will be able to speak, think and write critically and solve problems during your college career and beyond. All our graduates will demonstrate the ability to use technology to manage information and present that information effectively both in writing and through verbal presentations. CSUB graduates will be required to demonstrate proficiency in their major discipline. Our students will be able to apply discipline based knowledge to address real world problems and issues and they will know how they can prepare for careers in their chosen academic disciplines. Also, when our students graduate from CSUB, they will be able to demonstrate quantitative reasoning skills and utilize common mathematical calculations and estimations. In other words, all our graduates will possess numerical literacy. We feel that all of the preceding learning outcomes will be rendered meaningless unless our graduates use these skills to become active members of their communities who are engaged and ready to act independently and in groups to achieve desired results. Our graduates will have a good understanding of ethical frameworks; will have an appreciation for cultural and ethnic diversity; and will be well rounded.

I hope that you will enjoy the passage to graduation and, again, on behalf of this outstanding faculty, I offer you my support and best wishes.

Vandana Kohli

CALIFORNIA STATE UNIVERSITY, BAKERSFIELD
UNIVERSITY LEARNING OUTCOMES

Goal I. Students will show critical reasoning and problem solving skills.

    Objective 1A: The student will demonstrate the ability to read critically.

    Objective 1B: The student will demonstrate the ability to write critically.

    Objective 1C: The student will demonstrate the ability to speak critically.

    Objective 1D: The student will demonstrate the ability to think critically.

    Objective 1E: The student will demonstrate the capacity for life-long learning.

    Objective 1F: The student will engage in critical problem solving.

Goal II. Students will be able to communicate orally and in writing.

    Objective 2A: The student will present information in a professional manner using well-developed writing skills.

    Objective 2B: The student will present information in a professional manner using well-developed oral presentation skills.

    Objective 2C: The student will demonstrate competence in information management.

    Objective 2D: The student will demonstrate computer literacy.

Goal III. Students will demonstrate discipline-based knowledge and career-based-learning.

    Objective 3A: The student will demonstrate broad knowledge in their selected discipline.

    Objective 3B: The student will successfully apply discipline-based knowledge to the real world.

    Objective 3C: The student will successfully engage in career preparation and planning.

Goal IV. Students will possess numerical literacy.

    Objective 4A: The student will correctly utilize mathematical calculations and estimation skills.

    Objective 4B: The student will demonstrate quantitative reasoning skills.

    Objective 4C: The student will successfully apply quantitative reasoning skills to the real world.

Goal V. Students will become engaged citizens.

    Objective 5A: The student will engage in university and community activities (including civic action).

    Objective 5B: The student will demonstrate superior interpersonal skills.

    Objective 5C: The student will develop and demonstrate a thorough knowledge of self.

    Objective 5D: The student will demonstrate responsibility in group settings (including teamwork, leadership, managing skills, etc.)

    Objective 5E: The student will demonstrate the ability to work independently.

Goal VI. Students will develop a well rounded skill set.

    Objective 6A: The student will possess and demonstrate an ethical framework.

    Objective 6B: The student will demonstrate an understanding of cultural and ethnic diversity.

    Objective 6C: The student will successfully apply research methods/analysis and technology for problem solving.

    Objective 6D: The student will demonstrate interdisciplinary knowledge.

ROADRUNNER RESOURCES FOR UNDERGRADUATE SUCCESS AND HIGH-ACHEIVEMENT (RUSH-A)
PROGRAM OUTCOMES

Goal 1. Students will develop a clear understanding of the traditions, culture, role, and importance of higher education and how it figures into their long-term personal mission.

Outcome 1. Students will demonstrate an understanding of the history of CSUB and the Bakersfield/Kern county community.

Outcome 2. Students will be able to describe the differences between high school and university cultures and the new responsibilities they must assume as a college student.

Outcome 3. Students will demonstrate an understanding of their rights and responsibilities as a member of the CSUB community

Goal 2. Students will acquire knowledge for academic success, including technical skills and information literacy.

Outcome 1. Students will understand the need for lower-division prerequisites in their major

Outcome 2. Students will demonstrate an understanding of the necessity of completing remediation courses and how successful completion impacts collegiate-level course performance

Outcome 3. Students will be able to develop a plan for the completion of remediation during the first year and general education requirements in the first two years

Outcome 4. Students will be able to develop a plan for exploring majors, if undecided

Goal 3. Students will gain knowledge of CSUB and an understanding of how to access academic support services.

Outcome 1. Students will demonstrate the ability to identify and articulate the benefits of appropriate campus resources

Outcome 2. Students will demonstrate the ability to locate and access campus resources (physical location, hours of operation)

Goal 4. Students will become familiar with university policies and regulations.

Outcome 1. Students will describe the differences between high school and university organizational structures and how to utilize them.

Outcome 2. Students will demonstrate the ability to locate sources of the appropriate policies and regulations

Goal 5. Students will begin the process of increasing awareness of, and appreciation for, diverse cultures, values, and belief systems.

Outcome 1. Students will demonstrate an awareness of their own culture, values, and belief systems

Outcome 2. Students will demonstrate a respect for diverse points-of-view and the ability to engage in civil discourse

Goal 6. Students will become meaningfully involved in university life through connection and engagement with other students, faculty, staff, and administrators.

Outcome1. Students will understand the options available for campus engagement through clubs and organizations

Outcome 2. Students will recognize the opportunities for leadership and community service during their college career

Goal 7. Students will participate in the shared academic experience of a common reader.

Outcome 1. Students will engage in a community-wide experiential exercise in civil discourse on a timely topic through the *Runner Reader* Program

Outcome 2. Students will demonstrate the value of the life-long practice of reading to broaden one's horizons

Goal 8. Students will take an active responsibility for their own education by planning for future personal success at CSUB.

Outcome 1. Students will demonstrate an improvement in technical and academic skills (such as note-taking, critical reading, writing, speaking and thinking, problem solving, and presentation skills)

Outcome 2. Students will demonstrate an understanding of the General Education pattern at CSUB (i.e., American Institutions, Areas, Themes)

CSUB On-Line

It is easier than ever to access the many faces of CSUB through electronic media!

The "CSUB Blog" (http://csubblog.wordpress.com/) addresses Runner related educational news. There are also numerous Facebook pages devoted to CSUB. Here are some fine options to become an active part of CSUB's online presence through Facebook:

Would you like to learn more about the food options and issues related to CSUB? Join the "CSUB Dining" group.

Want to improve your math skills or meet others who love math? Join the "Math CSUB" page, a Facebook page devoted to Mathematics and Statistics.

If you are thinking of going into education, you may want to join the "CSUB Educational Counseling" site.

Would you like to keep current on all the Student Rec Center news? Join the "CSUB Student Recreation Center" group.

Do you want to help others? Find out many options for doing so through the "Community Service Cooperative CSUB" group.

The "ASI CSUB" page will keep you up to date on all the Associated Students issues.

If you are a sports fanatic, the CSUB Roadrunners, CSUB Softball, or the CSUB Judo Force Group may be for you. You could also visit www.gorunners.com to learn all about CSUB athletics.

Once you have graduated, you will definitely need to keep contact with all your CSUB friends through the CSUB Alumni Facebook page.

CSUB Facebook

Most importantly, if you are a Facebook member, you should join the general CSUB Facebook group. Sign in to your Facebook account and search for CSUB. Join the main CSUB Facebook group. In doing so, you are helping us "to become the leading campus in the CSU system in terms of academic excellence, diversity, quality and community engagement."

An Evening With
WES MOORE

Author of
THE OTHER WES MOORE

TUESDAY, NOVEMBER 8, 2011
7:00 P.M. • CSUB ICARDO CENTER
Book Discussion • Q&A • Book Signing

THIS EVENT IS FREE AND OPEN TO THE PUBLIC.
Free Parking in Lot I after 6:00 p.m.

Presented by One Book, One Bakersfield, One Kern, The CSUB First-Year Experience Program, Associated Students, Inc., the Department of English and Sigma Tau Delta

Wes Moore

What is it like to be in combat in Afghanistan; to speak at the Democratic National Convention; to appear on Meet the Press, The Oprah Winfrey show, and the Colbert Report; to graduate Phi Beta Kappa from Johns Hopkins; to receive a White House Fellowship under Condoleeza Rice; to study in England as a Rhodes scholar; to grow up fatherless and poor in Baltimore? You'll find out when you read Wes Moore's account in *The Other Wes Moore*.

What is like to share a name with someone whose life has gone in a completely different direction? When Wes Moore learns of another man with the same name, from the same neighborhood, he begins to explore the ways that lives can develop so differently: one Wes Moore becomes a business and community leader while the other Wes Moore serves a life sentence for murder in Maryland's Jessup Correctional Institution.

You will also learn about Wes Moore when you read this year's Runner Reader selection, *The Other Wes Moore*. Now a global strategist for Citigroup, the author lives in Manhattan with his family. *The Other Wes Moore* is truly the story of a man who took "the road less traveled." When you read his account and hear his presentation, you'll see what a difference a few simple decisions can make.

20 Questions for Wes Moore

E-mail Emerson Case (ecase@csub.edu) with questions you would like Wes Moore to answer. He will respond to

In conjunction with the Li'i Pearl Writing Awards:
The CSUB Roadrunner First-Year RUSH-A Program
Runner Reader Essay Contest

Do you like writing? Do you like sharing your insights? Do you like competing for prizes?

Then enter **The *Runner Reader* Essay Contest**.

The winners will be revealed during Moore's campus visit on November 8th, 2011

Prizes:

1st place:	$250
2nd place	$150
3rd place	$100

This Year's Topic

One of Robert Frost's most famous poems is *The Road Not Taken* in which the speaker describes one choice as having "made all the difference" in defining his life.

Using the experience of both Wes Moores, explain how one choice can define a person's life, and argue whether —and how— a person can transcend that definition.

You may use personal examples as well as examples from history and other sources, but you must use Moore's text as a foundation.

Essay Contest Guidelines

To be eligible, you must be a matriculated student in CSUB 101, CSUB 301, ENGLISH 80, ENGLISH 100 or ENGLISH 110.

A written essay is the only literary form accepted (no poems, plays, songs, etc.).

Only one essay may be submitted by each contestant.

Each essay should reflect the contestant's own interpretation and original thinking.

Each contestant must complete and submit a contest entry form which requires your teacher's signature for verification of authenticity.

The contestant's name should only appear on the entry form and should not appear on any page of the essay.

The title of the essay, but not the contestant's name, must appear on the top of the first page of the essay text.

Completed submissions should be turned in to your teacher.

- The essay should be between 2 and 4 pages long.
- The essay must be submitted typed, double-spaced on one side of the page only.
- Use 12-point font (preferably Times New Roman or Arial).
- Use 1-inch margins all around.
- Do not justify the right margin.
- Pages should be sequentially numbered.
- Use MLA-style documentation when quoting from the book.
- The essay should be bound by a single staple in the upper left-hand corner (Do not use a binder or folder). Do not staple the entry form to the essay.

By entering the contest, you confirm that the essay submission is your own original creation. The essays will be judged by a committee of CSUB faculty, staff and students. The winners will be announced during the author's visit on November 8th, 2011. Contest winners agree to allow their essays to be posted on the Roadrunner First-Year RUSH-A Program web-site.

Entries must be received <u>by your teacher</u> by October 21, 2011

Essays will be judged on the following criteria:

Creativity – Does the essay reflect a creative and original perspective on the book?

Organization – Does the argument follow a logical and easily understood progression?

Clarity – Does the author use concise language?

Unity/Development of thought– Does the essay reflect a thorough comprehension of the symbols and themes of the book?

Grammar/Mechanics – Does the contestant use correct grammar, spelling, and punctuation?

Entry forms can be found online at
http://www.csub.edu/Rush-A/Essay_Contest_Entry_Form.htm

Chapter One: College Expectations

Many students equate a college education with job training. This, however, is false equivocation. A university does not exist to prepare students for the workforce. In fact, the word "college" comes from the Latin *collegium*, meaning community; "university" comes from *universus*, meaning the whole, the universe. In each case, the foundations of college and university refer to a community, a group of individuals creating a whole. How does this apply to you? When you come to a college or university, you are expected to join this community, to become part of the whole.

Thus, you are neither a passive audience member meant to be informed and entertained nor an empty slate meant to be programmed for future work. Rather, you are here as part of a collaboration— a system of students, professors, administrators, and staff—that works to advance knowledge.

Looking to One's Career

For most students, a university education is a step in a process that leads to a fulfilling career. In fact, the college degree is often a prerequisite for many companies. What many students do not know, however, is that it is not the degree itself that the companies desire; it is what that degree represents. In fact, many Fortune 500 companies go out of their way to hire graduates with Philosophy and Psychology degrees and not necessarily those who have degrees in Business or Economics.

What, then, do these companies desire in their employees that a college degree represents?

The diploma represents a body of knowledge, and that "body" is intended to be both wide (your general education) and deep (your major and minor). An employee who has a wide body of knowledge has a pool of information he or she can access as the need arises.

The diploma also represents an individual's persistence and diligence. A diploma represents years of struggle and focus and signifies your ability to succeed in the face of adversity and challenge. Society expects a college education to be demanding, and so students should expect to be challenged intellectually at every turn.

Your College Experience

There are many similarities between high school and college. Just as in high school, college is filled with a routine of teachers, classes, and homework. Unfortunately, many students make the mistake of equating high school with college, and they continue to think and act as though they are still in high school.

This is a recipe for disaster.

High school contains an infrastructure designed to transition students from being children to being adults. Consequently, high school teachers, counselors, and administrators are there to continuously monitor and advise students on assignments, grades, and extracurricular activities. Colleges and universities, on the other hand, assume their students are adults and treat them as such. Thus, it is the student's responsibility to man-

age his or her own time, class schedule, and college workload. A college professor will not notify you that you are failing the class; a college professor will not remind you that the essay is due in two days; and a college professor will not accept "my printer ran out of ink" as an excuse for not having an assignment on the day it is due.

The university does have a support system for students that includes tutoring centers, advisors, and health centers, but it is the student's responsibility to seek these out and take advantage of them: you must know where and whom to ask for help.

Classroom Tips and Strategies

Success in college is dependent on more than essay and test scores; it requires a pattern of thinking and behavior that allows you to acquire and digest information. This pattern is most visible in the classroom. Here are some strategies that will help you:

1. Be on time to class.
2. Be prepared when you come to class: read the text, and come with questions.
3. Sit close to the front, and take notes.
4. Ask questions both in class and during your instructor's office hours.
5. Complete your work on time, and make sure your work meets the instructor's requirements.
6. Review your syllabus before and after class each day.
7. Avoid interrupting class with personal issues; these should be discussed during the instructor's office hours.

Campus Civility

Civility is the hallmark of a healthy society, a functioning civilization, but what does it mean to be civil?

Civility is a form of respect; it is a respect for other individuals, but it is also a respect for the social codes and structures in which we communicate and interact.

Civility is essential to the university setting because a university is a living repository of conflicting ideas, values, and philosophies. In such an environment, an uncivil atmosphere leads to conflict and dysfunction. A civil atmosphere, on the other hand, facilitates greater communication, insight, and growth.

Being civil does not mean agreeing with every opinion and argument others make.

Being civil does mean giving those individuals the opportunity to present those opinions and arguments without the fear of being shouted down, disrespected, or insulted.

How to Annoy Your Instructor: Be Uncivil

- *Arrive to class late, or leave class early.*

- *Finish your math homework during your psychology class.*

- *Text message your friends while you're in class.*

- *Sit in the back and chat with your friends.*

- *Yawn loudly, or fall asleep.*

- *Fix your hair or makeup in class.*

- *Skip class and then ask the professor, "Did I miss anything important?"*

Etiquette at Public Events

One purpose of this book is to encourage you to participate more actively in the many public offerings that CSUB provides. There will be hundreds of opportunities to see plays, musicals, operas, chamber musicians, and solo artists.

When you do go to these events, or to any public event, you must follow the proper etiquette:

1. do not put your feet on the back of the seat in front of your;

2. never show up late or leave early;

3. by all means, turn off your cell phone or texting device; furthermore, do not text at all during an event;

4. reserve conversations until later as talking during a show is rude and offensive;

5. finally, do not eat or drink during the event.

On several occasions, student audiences have been incredibly ill-mannered to our performers by violating the previously stated rules. Obviously, these are simple rules of etiquette. Imagine being on stage yourself; you would want an attentive and respectful audience.

Grades

High School	College
1. Grades are given for most assigned work.	1. Grades may not be given for all work. Sometimes, there will only be a check, and sometimes, the instructor may not collect the work at all.
2. Consistent attendance often equates with passing grades.	2. Attendance is expected. Consistent attendance will not by itself raise your scores.
3. Consistently good homework scores will make up for low test or essay scores.	3. Most college courses are weighed heavily towards a few assignments or exams.
4. Teachers often grade on the curve, and this curve will likely raise grades for everyone.	4. Professors rarely grade on the curve.
5. Teachers often offer extra credit.	5. Professors rarely offer extra credit.
6. A "D" is good enough to pass the course.	6. Many courses require a grade of "C" or better.
7. Teachers often give credit to a student's "effort" if that student has "tried hard."	7. Professors grade on results.

Essays

High School	College
1. Teachers often assign essays in stages, with the instructor commenting on each stage.	1. Professors usually assign final drafts, with the professor grading the final work.
2. Teachers often remind you when the essay is due and how far along you should be in the process of writing.	2. It is your responsibility to complete the essay on time, and professors will rarely remind you.
3. Teachers are often forgiving as to variations in font size, grammar, and mechanics; you're graded on your ideas.	3. Professors expect you to follow conventions of writing style, in terms of font, grammar, and mechanics; you are graded on your ideas as well as the structure of those ideas.
4. Teachers often offer re-writes.	4. Professors rarely allow re-writes.

Exams

High School	College
1. Testing is frequent and covers a small amount of material.	1. Testing is cumulative and covers a large amount of material; in some classes, there will only be one exam.
2. Teachers often provide a study guide, sometimes with the same questions that will be on the exam.	2. Professors rarely provide study guides; it is your responsibility to create your own study guide.
3. Teachers often devote class time to reviewing for the exam.	3. Professors rarely devote class time to review; it is your responsibility to form study groups.
4. Teachers often offer make-up exams.	4. Professors rarely offer make-up exams.
5. Teachers often offer extra credit to make up for a student's low test score.	5. Professors rarely offer extra credit of any kind.

Freedom and Responsibility

High School

1. Most of your classes are arranged for you.

2. Counselors will make sure you meet the requirements for graduation.

3. Others manage your time for you, and there are relatively few distractions.

4. Teachers and parents will remind you of deadlines and obligations.

College

1. You are responsible for your class schedule.

2. Advisors will help you meet the requirements for graduation, but it is your responsibility to make appointments with your advisor, and it is your responsibility to make sure you meet graduation requirements.

3. You are responsible for managing your time, and there will be an endless number of potential distractions.

4. You must balance your own responsibilities and obligations.

Your College / University Professor

- Professors are usually open and helpful, but they expect you to initiate contact if you need assistance; this is the purpose of an instructor's office hours.

- Professors expect you to read your syllabus carefully; the syllabus contains class expectations and requirements. Don't ask a professor a question the syllabus already answers.

- Professors may not follow the textbook. Often, a professor will use his or her lecture to supplement the information in the text.

- Professors expect you to get notes from classmates when you are absent.

- Professors may lecture for the entire class session; it is your responsibility to take effective notes.

- Professors expect you to participate in class discussions.

- Professors expect you to ask questions during class.

- Professors expect you to synthesize information and make connections.

- Professors may not take attendance, but they will know who has been attending their classes.

High School Administration ~ University Academic Affairs

In high school, your principal or vice principal can answer most, if not all, of your questions and can solve most of your problems. In high school, the administration is strictly hierarchical, with the principal at the top. Colleges and universities, on the other hand, have a more complex system of academic affairs that a student must know how to navigate if he or she has academic questions or concerns.

If a student has questions regarding a class, the student should ask the instructor or professor first. If the student still has concerns, he or she should direct them to the Department Chair. CSUB also has an ombudsman, Janet Millar, who serves to facilitate dialogue between students and the University when help is needed to resolve a disagreement or misunderstanding. The Ombudsperson does not impose solutions, but acts as a neutral mediator in problems-solving and conflict resolution. Problems that have been brought to the Ombudsperson have involved access to facilities, grading policies, disputes about fees, conflicts between students and instructor/staff, and disciplinary matters.

These and other issues can be discussed with the Ombudsperson who will listen to you, provide information and assist in identifying the options available to you.

All contacts, records and communications with Ombudsperson are confidential within State laws and CSU policies.

Students wishing to consult with the Ombudsperson may make an appointment by calling the Counseling Center (661) 654-3366. Monday-Friday 8 a.m. to 5 p.m. Special hours can be arranged.

Misconceptions about College and University Life

Many students are shocked when they realize that what they thought they knew about college turns out not to be true:

1. *College is job training.* This is perhaps the most common misconception people have about college. While you will learn skills that are transferable to the business world, that is not the purpose of a college education. Rather, college is designed to provide a well-rounded liberal education wherein a student is exposed to and synthesizes information from diverse fields and perspectives. A college graduate is an individual who can see and think outside and beyond "the box." Likewise, a successful college student is one who has contributed to the on-going discussion and debate with something new and original; a person who has memorized information and dates but has little understanding or insight into how or why that information is significant is a person who has not taken advantage of his or her college experience.

2. *Once I finish a class, I'm done with that subject.* Again, the purpose of a college education is to enable you to make your own connections that go beyond what you may learn in any one individual class. For example, you could apply theories of trauma you learned about in your Psychology class to a poem you're reading in your English class or to the political structures of post World-War II Japan you're studying in Modern History. The point of learning is that it never stops, and you never know when a connection will click into place. Who knows? You may be the first to have seen that connection, and that could be the key to your future career.

3. *A college diploma will ensure that I get a great-paying job when I graduate.* While it is true that on average a college graduate will earn more money over his or her lifetime than a non-college graduate, there is no gold-plated office waiting for you when you graduate. With more and more people graduating from college, it is imperative that you offer skills those other college graduates lack. Many positions will have a college diploma as a prerequisite, but that by no means ensures that you will be the one individual out of the four-hundred-fifty applicants with a college diploma who gets the job. Similarly, many positions that require a college diploma are not well-paid. The individuals who pursue these positions do so for reasons other than joining the upper tax brackets; they may be working to help others, to advance knowledge, or to express themselves creatively.

On-Line Courses

At first thought, taking on-line courses may sound like an easy way to take a class. The reality is that on-line courses may be even more academically challenging than taking a course in a classroom because there are no immediate incentives for you to stay on task. In an on-line course, no one knows that you did not pay attention to a lecture or that you failed to complete your reading assignments. That is, until you take your first test! Below are some important tips to help you succeed in your on-line course:

1. **Designate a regular "study time."** Treat the on-line course just like your face-to-face courses. Set aside a few hours several times a week for your course. This will get you accustomed to the on-line learning process as well as provide you with a regular schedule. Tell your friends and families about this "study time" so that they will not interrupt you. Stick to this schedule so that you keep up with your assignments and lectures. Once you fall behind, especially in the quarter system, it becomes difficult to catch up.

2. **Designate a "study area."** This can be anywhere where you have access to a computer, but remember it should be a quiet place free of distractions. Clear the area or desk only with material for the course otherwise you may be tempted to work on other course work.

3. **Keep a calendar of assignments.** Meet all your deadlines. On the first day of the quarter, go over your syllabus and write down your assignment due dates on a calendar. This is very important! You may have the best intentions of remembering to complete all of your assignments and homework on time, but as the quarter progresses you will get busy in your other courses. A calendar will keep you on track.

4. **Keep your notes organized.** Even thought it is an on-line course and you are not attending a lecture, you will still need to take notes for your online courses. Keep all your notes in the same place either in a notebook or in a computer file.

5. **Meet your classmates.** If you can, get a list of your classmates from your professor. You can set up virtual study sessions, ask each other questions, and discuss assignments. You don't have to actually meet them in person, but interacting with your classmates through email, instant messaging, or web cam feeds will make your schooling experience much richer.

6. **Meet your professor and attend office hours.** If you are having difficulties in the course, contact your professor. First send an email introducing yourself and request an appointment.

Building Life Skills: Planning Your Time

SLEEP: How much sleep do you need each week? Number of hours of sleep each night x 7 nights/week =

TOTAL _____

ENTERTAINMENT/RELAXATION: How many hours per week do you normally watch television, socialize with friends, relax, play video games, etc?

TOTAL _____

COMMUTING: How much time do you spend each week commuting to campus and/or to a job?

TOTAL _____

EMPLOYMENT: How many hours per week do you work on- or off-campus at a paid or volunteer job?

TOTAL _____

VOLUNTEER ACTIVITIES: In addition to the hours listed above, how many hours per week do you devote to volunteer activities (church, tutoring, etc)?

TOTAL _____

MEALS: How many hours per week do you spend preparing food, eating meals, washing the dishes, etc?

TOTAL _____

CHORES: How long does it take you to complete your chores (doing laundry, washing the car, buying groceries, cleaning house) each week?

TOTAL _____

EXTRACURRICULAR ACTIVITIES: What about sports (e.g., soccer practice, working out), clubs (Judo Club, political groups), fraternities, or sororities? How much time per week?

TOTAL _____

CLASSES AND LABS: How much time are you required to be in class each week (including lab times)?

TOTAL _____

HOURS REQUIRED FOR STUDY: Your outside-of-class study time should be at least triple the number of hours listed in the "Classes and Labs" category above (e. g., 15 hours of class time per week times three equals 45 hours of study time.) No cheating on this answer!

TOTAL _____

STUDY GROUPS: Are you a member of any special study groups? If so, how many hours per week?

TOTAL _____

OTHER COMMITMENTS

TOTAL _____

- -

TOTAL ALLOCATED TIME PER WEEK

TOTAL _____

NOW SUBTRACT YOUR TOTAL HOURS FROM 168, THE NUMBER OF HOURS IN A WEEK, TO ARRIVE AT YOUR FREE TIME

TOTAL _____

Suggestions for Scheduling Your Time

A good schedule can help immensely in making your time in college more efficient, pleasurable, and worry-free. Far from turning you into a robot, a schedule liberates you from making constant decisions, thereby allowing you to have the best possible use of your time.

Here are some specific suggestions about constructing a schedule:

- *Most highly successful people habitually plan their day at a regular time, spending five or ten minutes in the morning or just before bedtime the night before going over their daily schedule.*

- *Allow larger blocks of time for learning new material, grasping new concepts, writing a paper, etc. Divide these large blocks of time into definite sub-periods that comfortably match the length of your concentration span (10 minutes? 20 minutes? 30 minutes?). As you begin work on each sub-period, jot down the time you expect to be finished. When you have completed each task, reward yourself with a brief break, a snack, or some other pleasurable activity . . . whatever makes you happy.*

- *Use short periods of time (15 to 30 minutes) to review. Make it a habit to spend a few minutes reviewing your notes immediately before each class meeting and then again right after class.*

- *Schedule harder tasks when you are alert and concentrating well. Study for your toughest courses first; then move on to the other classes.*

- *Spend at least 10 minutes reviewing each subject every day. Don't let your assignments pile up. The quarter system moves like lightning!*

- *If you get confused, frustrated, or just plain lost, ask your professors for help immediately. Helping you succeed is their most important job!*

- *Studies show that 15 hours per week is the maximum amount of time you can spend on an outside job without a negative impact on your grades. Ask yourself these questions: Do I really need all that extra money? Or are my studies more important? Don't let your employers suck the life out of you by demanding that you work longer and longer hours.*

- *Don't forget to allow time for fun and relaxation. You deserve it! All work and no play makes for a dull student.*

—Dr. Michael Flachmann, Director of University Honors Programs
English Department

CSUB-Antelope Valley

Do you live in the high desert?

Did you know that CSUB has a campus in the beautiful Antelope Valley?

With over nine undergraduate degree programs and eleven post-baccalaureate options, CSUB-AV is here for you now! CSUB-AV offers advisors to help with the choice of your major and courses, tutoring services, computer labs, library services, and health services.

The First-Year Experience: Explore Your Possibilities

The First-Year Experience program is a year-long set of courses (CSUB 101, 103, 105) designed to help you effectively transition from high school to CSUB, to help you find your place at CSUB, to help you know your faculty better, and to help you explore and understand CSUB's resources and services.

Psychologist Carl Jung uses the term "individuation" to describe the process of developing and realizing the potential of one's inner self. A CSUB education entails studying and becoming knowledgeable in academic fields, but it also includes your inner journal of realizing and actualizing your full potential as a scholar, a citizen, and a human being.

The First-Year Experience exists to encourage and facilitate that discovery.

The First-Year Experience Center is in Administration East 101 and offers a computer lab where students can conduct research or write essays, a study area where students can meet for group study sessions, and a lounge where students can relax between classes. Take advantage of this resource that exists to help you!

Chapter Two:
Information Literacy

Much of this chapter comes courtesy of Sarah Philips, the CSUB librarian specializing in the First Year Experience.

Distributing Information Electronically

Thanks to ongoing advances in technology, the process of teaching and learning is undergoing substantial changes in the distribution of materials. Whereas in the past, professors would mimeograph or photocopy syllabi and readings for the class, now much of that distribution occurs electronically.

The first setting for this information is the instructor's homepage; this is where you may find class information (including syllabi and assignment descriptions) as well as information about the instructor's office hours and contact information. Many professors include their professional information here as well, so you can see just what your professor does when he or she isn't teaching. You can find your professor's webpage by searching the Faculty Web Directory at http://www.csub.edu/search.html.

Many professors also use an electronic course management system called Blackboard. Unlike a webpage, the information given through Blackboard is available only to those who are registered in the specific class. For information as to how to access your Blackboard account or reset your password, go to E-Learning Services (www.csub.edu/els).

Finally, many professors create their own e-mailing lists and send information to students directly through e-mail. This information may concern changes to the syllabus, or the professor may e-mail the class to let the students know that class has been cancelled.

Because your professor may send you information at any time, it is a good idea to check your e-mail and Blackboard account (if your class uses it) at least once a day.

Walter Stiern Library

The library's homepage http://www.csub.edu/library/) is the portal to the library's information resources. It is accessible from any computer connected to the Internet. From the homepage, you can gain access to the book catalog, online reference sources, research databases and more than 20,000 full-text electronic periodicals (journals, magazines and newspapers). If you are off campus, you will be prompted for your CSUB login information to gain access to the databases.

Walter Stiern Library: The Main Level

On the main level, you will find the Check Out Desk and the Reference Desk as well as all of the librarian's offices and the Reference Area computers, which are available for you to work on whenever the library is open. These reference computers provide access to the Internet and have the latest version of Microsoft Office but do not have any other programs.

When you first enter the Walter Stiern Library, you will see the Check Out Desk on your left. At the Check Out Desk, also called the Circulation Desk, you can check out books or course reserves and make a request for a video or DVD from the library collection. A valid CSUB Runner ID Card is required for all checkouts. Please return items at the Check Out Desk, in the drop box in Parking Lot D, or in the drop box by the front door of the library. Staff at the Check Out Desk can also assist you with photocopiers and media viewing equipment (the TV, DVD and VHS players) on the 2nd floor. Refunds for money lost in photocopiers and printers are also given at the Check Out Desk. The library lost and found is kept at the Check Out Desk and unclaimed high value items are sent to the University Police Department.

You can call the Check Out Desk for assistance any time the library is open: 661-654-3172

Many interesting resources are also found on the main level, including the First Year Experience Collection, the popular Fiction collection, the Multicultural Collection, Reference and Government Publication Collections.

The Dezember Reading Room is perhaps the most comfortable room on campus and contains a selection of current newspapers, magazines, and journals as well as a few popular collections of books, including the Multicultural Collection, the Bestseller Collection, and the First Year Experience Collection. The books in the First Year Experience Collection cover topics including how to pick a major, how to develop good study habits, how to maintain healthy personal relationships,

and how to give effective presentations. Many books in this collection relate to the common reader (*Burro Genius*).

IRTS stands for Information Resource Technology Services and exists to maintain and support technology across campus. The staff here can help you when you have problems with your computer or flash drive or when you have software questions.

Even when the Walter Stiern Library is closed, sometimes you can use the 24 Hour Study Room or the large computer lab on the lower level. Using your current ID card, you can access the lower level of the building via the glass doors on the west side.

Walter Stiern Library: Other Levels

On the lower level of the library, you may have classes in one of the computer labs or you can study in Lab A, or in the 24-Hour Room, which is open 24 hours a day during the school year.

On the second floor, you can watch DVDs, videos, or listen to CDs in the multimedia viewing area; the second floor also houses print periodicals (magazines, newspapers and journals) and a photocopy room.

Photocopies and Printing

The library has two photocopy rooms: one is behind the Reference Area computers on the east side of the Main level and the other is on the 2nd floor next to the elevators. Copies and printing cost $.15 per page and are black and white only. You pay by adding money to your Runner ID Card in Lab A or in the Copy Room on the 2nd floor.

Computer Labs

The Open Use lab, also referred to as Lab A, is in the lower level of the library. Lab A contains 82 computers for walk-in, open use by students, faculty, and staff of CSUB. There are 61 PC and 20 Macintosh workstations, as well as an ADA-compliant PC workstation.

You can have your ID picture taken and pick up your Runner ID in Lab A, and Lab A is one of the two places in the library that you can add money to your Runner ID card.

Hours for Lab A can be found at:
http://www.csub.edu/library/hours.shtml

On the 3rd and 4th floors of the library, you will find the Main Collection which holds most of our books and group study rooms.

Many students need a quiet place to focus on their coursework where they will not be distracted. The 24-hour study room on the Main Level and Lower Level of the Library is open throughout the school year except for major holidays. The north side of the first through fourth floors have large tables intended for quiet study. The group study rooms on the third and fourth floors are available for students to work collaboratively and not disturb others.

Color Copies & Media Equipment

You can make color copies and transparencies as well as use the scanners in the Multimedia Lab (654-2488) on the lower level of the library behind Lab A on the north side of the lower level. If you would like to borrow a video camera or other equipment, you would go to Media Services (654-2391).

Building Life Skills: Conducting Research

Why is using library resources more efficient than searching Google?

When you are looking for information online, where do you go? Google? Yahoo? Ask.com? Most likely your first response is to open up your favorite Internet Search Engine. Although Google can help us find out which movie theater is playing the newest Will Smith movie, it is not the best source for finding academic information.

It is common to feel overwhelmed by information. You may get dozens of e-mails, text messages, and phone calls from friends and family in one day. Instructors ask you to read books and articles. The more MySpace and Facebook friends you have, the more messages to which you are asked to respond.

The Internet is filled with junk: outdated pages, dead links, and inaccurate information. Using Google or Wikipedia may lead you to some results, but you can rarely be sure of their accuracy. What's more, you'll only be searching a fraction of all of the resources available to you. Library resources will direct you to scholarly, authoritative information that you can use for your assignments. Taking the time to learn how to use library resources now will help you save time with larger assignments in the future. Instead of spending your time trying to figure out if a website is acceptable, you can spend your time organizing and writing your paper.

While in college, you will need to research information for your homework, papers and projects. Once you graduate you will likely be expected, by your employer, to select the best information and make informed decisions. If you give your boss information that you found on a website that turns out to be fake, your job may be in jeopardy. The skills you develop while learning how to research will make finding information for your assignments, your job and your life much easier.

Finding Your Topic

One skill that you will need to master to be successful is to learn how to define your topic. As you learn more about your research topic, you will need to refine (either expand or narrow) your topic.

For example, if your Political Science or Feminism class asked you to write a paper on gender and geopolitics, you would want to begin by thinking about something that is interesting to you and summarizing the topic in a sentence, being as specific as possible:

I want to learn more about the role of women in Iran.

The next step is to identify the essential concepts or ideas.

Underline or circle the main concepts. Concepts are the different ideas which make up each unique search topic.

Most topics can be broken down into two or three main concepts.

I want to learn more about the role of women in Iran.

It will be useful to use other forms of your keywords, for example "woman" or "Iranian."

Finally, it will be useful to keep in mind synonyms or other terms related to your key words.

For example, concepts related to "women" include

feminine, female, gender, sex.

Concepts related to "Iran" could include *middle-east, Persian, Islamic.*

Finding a Book

After you have selected your keywords, you can search for books or articles that you might find interesting or useful. Unlike Google's single search box, library databases require you to separate your concepts into separate boxes. For your first search, you will use your keywords to find a book.

Type women into the first box and Iran into the second box. The catalog will automatically assume that you want to combine these two terms and will select "AND" between them. Press "Search Now."

The resulting list will include books or videos with your keywords in the Title or the general subject of the item. If you see a title that looks interesting, you will need to write down the Call Number and the Location to find it.

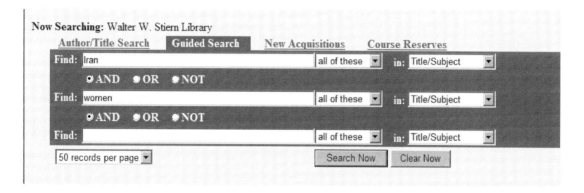

Our search has found 42 books, the first two of which are shown below. For more information on each book, including the author, table of contents, and other information, you would click on the title. To actually find the book, you need to take note of the call numbers. According to the citation, the book is found on Level 3 or 4. The key is to look at the first letter of the citation. Books with call numbers that begin with A-L are on the 3rd Floor; books that begin with M-Z are on the 4th Floor. Since our book begins with G, we would look on the 3rd Floor.

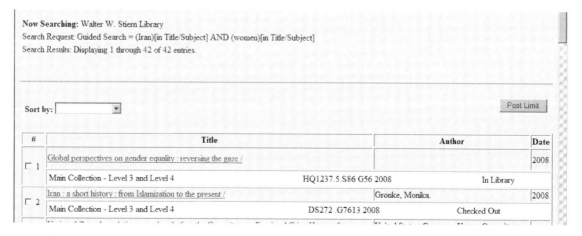

Finding a Scholarly Article

Although books are a good way to start your research because you can get a broad understanding of a topic, you will need to be able to find articles for your coursework. Our library features databases by subject, which makes it easier for you to narrow your search.

A good database for general research is Academic Search Elite, which is also known as part of Ebscohost.

By clicking on the title of the article, you can see more information including the Abstract (summary of the article) and descriptive keywords about the article. If you decide that this is an article that you would like to see the full-text of, you can either click on "PDF Full Text", "HTML Full Text" or "Check for Full Text".

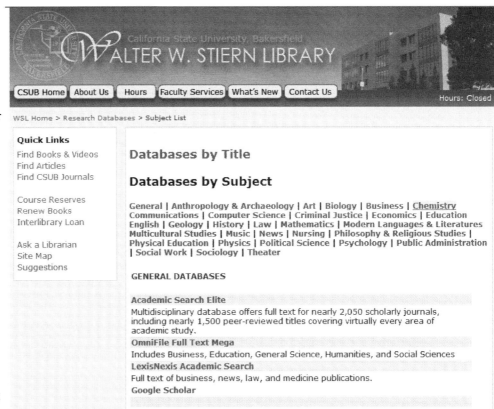

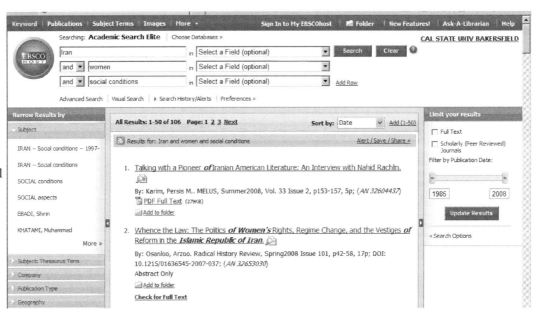

Individualized Research Assistance

The Walter W. Stiern Library offers individualized research assistance to help CSUB students identify resources for their research projects. For help with your research, you can schedule an appointment with a librarian who specializes in your subject area. The following lists librarians' subject areas, telephone numbers, room numbers and email addresses.

Johanna Alexander
jalexander@csub.edu
WSL 104, 654-3256

Business, Economics, Public Administration, Law

Curt Asher
casher@csub.edu
WSL 116F, 654-3251

History, Modern Languages & Literatures, Philosophy & Religious Studies, Physical Education

------

Christy Gavin
cgavin@csub.edu
WSL 116D, 654-3237

Anthropology, Archaeology, Art, Communications, English, Music, Social Work, Sociology, Theater

------

Kristine Holloway
kholloway2@csub.edu
WSL 116B, 952-5072, 654-3252

Education

Norm Hutcherson
nhutcherson@csub.edu
WSL 116C, 654-2061

Geology, Physics, Political Science, Psychology

Sarah Philips
sphilips@csub.edu
WSL 105, 654-3260

Criminal Justice, Multicultural Studies

Ying Zhong
yzhong@csub.edu
WSL 116G, 654-3119

Biology, Chemistry, Computer Science, Mathematics, Nursing,

Take a Research Class for Credit

There are courses offered each quarter which will help you develop your research skills. GST 126, GST 151, GST 153 and INST 420 are all taught by librarians and are designed to make you an expert searcher. These courses are all worth 2 credits and range in topic from "Research on the Internet" to "Electronic Legal Research." If you need 2 extra units that will help you prepare for college research, consider taking one of the Library's General Studies courses.

Interlibrary Loan

When you need an item that the library does not have available for you, we can borrow it from another library for free! By visiting the Interlibrary Loan link on the library website, you can log in as a student and make a request for the books or articles that you need. Because we are borrowing these materials from other libraries, it is best to give yourself at least a week, if not 10 days, to receive them. You will receive an email when they have arrived and are ready for you to pick up in the library or download an electronic copy from the library website. If the library does not have the book you want let us get it for you from another library! Plan ahead and request any material that you need!

Academic Honesty

Plagiarism is defined as the use of another's ideas or words without giving credit to the original source. In other words, a plagiarizer tries to pass off another person's work as if it is his or her own.

In the academic world, it is required that authors be credited for their ideas, research and writing. Not to do so is to plagiarize, to intentionally or unintentionally take the ideas, words, or work of another without sufficiently acknowledging that such material is not your own. By plagiarizing, you are putting yourself at risk for punishments which can range from failing the assignment, to failing the course, to being administratively dismissed from the university.

Plagiarizing can be

1. Handing in someone else's work as your own.

2. Copying OR purchasing a pre-written paper and claiming it as your own.

3. Using paragraphs, sentences, phrases, words or ideas written by another without giving appropriate citation and credit.

4. Using data or statistics compiled by another without giving appropriate citation and credit.

5. Submitting the same, or essentially the same, paper or other assignment for credit in two different courses without receiving approval from the instructors of the affected courses.

Source: 2007-2009 CSUB Catalog, page 81

Turnitin.com

You should be prepared to use the Turnitin.com program in any number of courses while at CSUB, starting with this CSUB 101 course. According to their website, Turnitin.com is a powerful tool which checks your work against "billions of pages from both current and archived instances of the internet, millions of student papers previously submitted to Turnitin, and commercial databases of journal articles and periodicals."

The procedure for signing up for Turnitin is fairly simple. Your professor will provide you with the class ID number and password. When you are copying these in class, be sure to copy them precisely. You should not need to ask your professor for information that he or she already gave you in class or on a syllabus.

With the class id number and password, go to the website, Turnitin.com, and submit your paper. After entering your personal information, such as your email address, you will click on the "submit" button. You will then click "browse" so that you can upload the file from a flash drive or computer hard drive. It is as simple as that.

The program will then check your essay against other essays that have been submitted or published elsewhere. Turnitin does not check for proper citation format and it does not determine whether you have plagiarized. That is up to the instructor reading the Turnitin report. Your instructor will see if you have properly quoted and cited the material that needs to be noted.

When you check your submission, you will see a percentage and a color. The percentage indicates how much of your writing matches other writing that Turnitin.com has found. This does not necessarily indicate plagiarism, for you may have quoted the material correctly. However, you should pay attention to the color bar. A green bar indicates that most of the writing is your own, while a red bar indicates that most of the writing is from other sources. Since your work should be original, you should stay in the green range.

However, plagiarism refers to the lack of correct citation and documentation, which is unrelated to the percentage and color bar, so you will want to review your submission closely.

MyWritingLab

MyWritingLab is an online program designed to help you with writing, grammar, and mechanics necessary for persuasive, logical, and effective writing in any course. MyWritingLab helps you to not only practice these skills, but to also brush up on study skills, learn about research, and even submit a paper in any subject area to a tutor. Because this program is online, you can work at your own pace. For example, you can watch an explanation and work on practicing the skill as many times as you need. You may encounter this program in your English composition classes here at CSUB, and you may even encounter this program in multitude of non-English courses as well. CSUB values clear writing and effective communication, and this program can help you with both.

Humanities/Behavioral Sciences 277 and 477 is designed to help you with writing, grammar, and mechanics necessary for persuasive, logical, and effective writing in any lower- or upper-division course. HUM/ BEHS 277 is open to freshmen and sophomores, while 477 is open to juniors and seniors; this program uses MyWritingLab as well.

All you have to do is sign up for the course (see http://www.csub.edu/mwl for CRN numbers) and buy the required text—English Simplified, a grammar handbook packaged with a MyWritingLab code. Then, you work through the program at your own pace throughout the quarter, working on areas in whatever areas you need help in.

What's Included?

Research Tools/MySearchLab is a resource through which you can learn how to do research from picking a topic to re-searching and docu-menting. As part of Research Tools, you receive a subscription to Ebscohost Content Select, New York Times, Financial Times, and the Library Link. Ebscohost Content Select allows you to search Ebsco via both a keyword and subject area. Library link allows you to find scholarly websites in a specific topic area. Through Re-search Navigator, students can also learn more about MLA, APA, Chicago, and CBE documentation styles.

Study Skills

The study skills resource allows you to learn more about note taking, exam preparation, time management, and other similar topics.

Pearson Tutor Services/SmartThinking

This resource allows you to submit up to 6 papers (up to 15 pages long) on any subject and have personalized feedback from a person with a Master's or PhD in that subject area. The papers come back in approximately 24 hours.

For more information, visit CSUB's MyWritingLab page at http://www.csub.edu/mwl/277477.html

Building Life Skills: E-mail Etiquette

Far too often, when students e-mail their instructors, those e-mails are confusing (for the instructor) and embarrassing (for the student). An e-mail is a textual, often permanent, representation of you: your intelligence and your character. As such, it is in your best interest to present yourself well. How best to accomplish this?

As with any correspondence, your e-mail should include the crucial details. Often, a student will send an e-mail to an instructor but neglect to include his or her name or the specific class he or she is attending. Here is one such example (an actual case):

hello professor, I talked to kathy and she was wondering if u could squeeze me into your class because I have no english class and she said you would more than likely do it.

Your e-mail should also be free of grammatical or factual errors, ambiguities, or unintended implications; the e-mail also should take a measured tone, free of any hostilities.

Here is another such example (an actual case):

Dear Professor,
I was wondering how I did on my final paper because I received a D in the the class? This was the last class I needed to graduate and I am not sure if a D is passing? I have tried numerous attempts to contact you and make sure that my work was adequate for you? where did I go wrong? I passed my social worker exam so if I did not pass your class I can not get the job? so please e-mail me back as soon as you get this e-mail.

An e-mail should reflect a student's level of writing and discourse, and the numerous mistakes in grammar and mechanics in the e-mail already provide clues as to why the student may not have passed the class.

- Always fill in the Subject Line with the theme of your email
- Indicate the class name and section
- Make sure that your message is clear, for if your email is confusing, your issue will not be resolved as quickly
- Request a meeting in person if an issue is complicated
- Use proper spelling, grammar, and punctuation
- DO NOT TYPE IN ALL CAPS, which indicates that you are yelling, or in all lowercase letters, which indicates a lack of professionalism
- Treat your faculty with respect by using appropriate titles when you address them: Dr., Professor, Mr. or Ms.
- Make sure to double check that you are spelling their name correctly!
- Proofread before hitting "send"
- Do not use an unprofessional e-mail address like honeybun23@gmail.com
- If a professor has been helpful, send a brief e-mail to say "thank you"
- If you are angry about something, wait a couple of hours before you send an e-mail.

E-mail Assignment

Your assignment: Send an e-mail to your CSUB 101 instructor letting him or her know that you will be missing class on a day that an assignment is due.

Write your e-mail in such a way that you present a legitimate alternate means of submitting that assignment.

Chapter Three: Your Well-Being

For many students, college is a time of overwhelming opportunity. Not only is there a schedule of classes to attend, but there are friends to hang out with, people to date, and parties to attend. Besides all this, there are bills to pay, meetings to attend, family members to take care of, and jobs to find . . . And don't forget that eight page paper due next Friday.

With all of these stressors, is it any wonder that so many students struggle with juggling their duties and desires?

Though it sometimes can seem as though you are being crushed by these obligations, there are strategies and lifestyle decisions you can make in order to manage these freedoms, responsibilities, and distractions.

The first step is to acknowledge and identify your situation. What type of stress are you experiencing?

- Physical stress, such as fatigue or insomnia?

- Emotional stress, such as anxiety or depression?

- Financial stress, such as wondering how to pay your bills?

- Stress in relationships with family, roommates, friends or in dating?

- Stress in managing your time and obligations?

The purpose of this chapter is to give you strategies for dealing with each of these questions and to point you towards a support system here at CSUB that exists to help you.

Your Stressors

Each of us has our own unique stress threshold.

Some of us have no problem handling physical stress, but then we get overwhelmed when we try to balance our checkbook.

Others are completely calm in the midst of financial stressors but seem to get sick every quarter during finals.

Make a list of your personal stressors.

What situations cause you the most stress?

Which stressful situations do you handle most easily?

Managing Stress Levels and Staying in College

Only 15 to 25 percent of all college and university departures result from academic failure. In other words, 75 to 85 percent of students who leave college without their diploma do so for non-academic reasons. There are four "clusters" that lead to students leaving or dropping out of college: adjustment, difficulty, incongruence, and isolation.*

Adjustment refers to the ability to transition between high school and college. For many students, this is the first time they have been away from home, and academic demands coupled with a seemingly-chaotic schedule become overwhelming.

Difficulty refers to the higher standards of academic discipline that college requires. Many students did not develop necessary study habits and skills in high school and are unprepared for the more rigorous demands that college places upon them.

Both incongruence and isolation fall under the category of integration, which refers to the ability (or lack thereof) of the student to feel as if he or she is part of the college. If a student feels like he or she is a "stranger" on campus or in class, he or she is probably experiencing a lack of integration.

Incongruence refers to the degree to which the student feels the college is a "good fit" for his or her interests, goals, and needs. In other words, the student feels like the college is not meeting his or her expectations of what college should be like.

Isolation refers to the lack of meaningful connection between the student and other students, faculty, and staff. In other words, the student feels separated from the myriad "communities" that constitute a college.

Most students experience these difficulties in some degree, but there are strategies to help you overcome them.

*Tinto. *Leaving College: Rethinking the Causes and Cures of Student Attrition*. Chicago: Univ. of Chicago P. 1993.

People often find that soothing sights and sounds help them relieve their stress. CSUB offers many such relaxation nooks. One of the most calming is the koi pond that rests in the shadow of the Walter Stiern Library.

Your Physical Health

Most people are aware of the dreaded "freshman fifteen," which refers to the weight gain many students experience when they begin college life. What brings about this sudden change?

For one thing, many students experience a spike in their stress levels when they begin college, and an evolutionary response to stress is to consume more calories, which is why we often find ourselves eating more when we are faced with hardship. While this strategy may have been useful when we were confronted with social disintegration and possible famines, today it is more of a nuisance or distraction.

In addition to this weight gain, many freshmen students find themselves getting sick more often than they are used to; often, a student will battle a cold or flu for weeks.

It is no coincidence that many students likewise experience sleep problems, whether it is insomnia or constant fatigue. A number of studies have found that college students report at least twice as many sleep problems as the general population; this lack of sleep is especially disturbing considering that Rapid Eye Movement Sleep (REM) is linked to learning efficiency.*

As with the "freshmen fifteen," lingering illnesses and sleep problems are physiological effects of stress, and it is essential that students monitor their physical health in order to succeed in college, for a student who is physically healthy is a student who is much more likely to comprehend and synthesize information from class and ultimately earn higher grades.

*Brown and Buboltz, "Applying sleep research to University Students: Recommendations for Developing a Student Sleep Education Program." *Journal of College Student Development*, May/Jun. 2002.

During the Academic Year, the recreation center will be open 6:00-10:00 Monday through Friday, 8:00-8:00 on Saturday, and 10:00-10:00 on Sunday.

Building Life Skills: Managing Physical Stress

Managing physical stress requires a triumvirate strategy that focuses on sleep, exercise, and diet.

Based on multiple studies, a good night's sleep requires between seven to eight hours of sleep and cannot be "made up" on the weekend. Thus, the first step in managing physical stress is ensuring that you get at least seven hours of sleep each night.

The second step in managing stress is to maintain regular exercise habits. Studies have shown that while 65% of high school students participate in regular physical activity, that number drops to 38% of college students.* Considering that physical exercise improves mood, can be an effective antidepressant, and helps the body fight infections, it is important that you create a pattern of regular physical exercise. One of the best ways to keep to a consistent plan of exercise is to work out with friends. Here at CSUB, you have many exercise options: the Student Recreation Center, the Hillman Aquatic Center, racquet ball and tennis courts, the track, and the bike path that runs along Kern River.

The third step in managing stress is to maintain a healthy diet. Too often, college students skip meals and instead turn to high-fat and low-nutrition snacks. Making healthy food choices starts with eating breakfast, the meal many college students skip. A healthy nutrition plan would continue with a diet heavy on fruits and vegetables and light on meats and fats.

Finally, many students suffer from a constant state of dehydration, which is linked to both physical illness and mental fatigue, so it is essential that you drink plenty of water throughout the day.

The key for any successful strategy is make it a fit for you.

What type of exercise do you prefer? Non-competitive exercise, like bicycling or jogging? Competitive exercise, like tennis or basketball?

What kind of food do you prefer? All types of food can be made healthy, whether you prefer vegetarian burritos or vegetarian *Pad Thai*.

*Kilpatrick, et al. "College Students' Motivation for Physical Activity: Differentiating Men's and Women's Motives for Sport Participation and Exercise." *Journal of American College Health*, Sept. 2005.

Student Recreation Center

Take advantage of the Student Recreation Center, which features:

- 13,000 square foot fitness area equipped with 60 cardiovascular machines including treadmills, elliptical cross-trainers, exercise bikes, climbers, and rowing ergometers; free weight benches, barbells, dumbbells, plate-loaded weight equipment, variable resistance weight machines, core strength area, stretching area, and 24 LCD big screen televisions.

- Seven exercise rooms with specialized hardwood flooring, mirrors, padding, and sound system for a variety of classes such as aerobics, martial arts, and yoga.

- Dedicated room for Personal Trainer services and assessment.

- 3-court gymnasium, (two hardwood courts and one resilient rubber floor) for informal and intramural basketball, volleyball, badminton, indoor soccer, and floor hockey.

- Indoor 32-foot high climbing wall with separate bouldering rock.

- Indoor 3-lane suspended 1/10th of a mile jogging/walking track.

- Lighted outdoor sports field for informal, intramural, and student club activities like soccer, flag football, ultimate, and softball.

- Juice bar.

Your Emotional Health

Emotional stress can take many forms: confusion, frustration, anxiety, depression, and anger. When we are under emotional stress, our bodies release stress hormones such as cortisol that help us get through the stressful situation, but these same hormones depress the immune system, which is why we often get sick when we are under stress. What causes college students such stress? The list is long and varied: course work, family obligations, relationships, financial obligations, employment, and career path choices. As one example, a 2005 study found that lonely and socially-isolated freshmen had a weaker immune response than other students to the flu vaccine. In other words, there is a strong correlation (if not a causal relationship) between a person's emotional and physical well-being.*

Therefore, it is essential that you learn effective strategies for managing your own types and levels of emotional stress. Remember, it's normal to experience stress, and it's also normal to seek help.

*Pressman, et al. "Loneliness, Social Network Size and Immune Response to Influenza Vaccination in College Freshman." *Health Psychology* 24.3 (2005).

CSUB has many General Studies classes geared toward specific interests and needs. One such course, General Studies 128, is a two-unit class devoted to stress management. Besides teaching you how to deal with your own stress levels, the class will provide techniques and strategies as to how to deal with stress in general, which is especially useful information for anyone going into any of the helping professions, such as teaching.

Building Life Skills: Managing Emotional Stress

When confronted with stressful situations, people tend to cope in one of two ways; either they focus on their emotional response or they focus on their problem. Both strategies can be effective, but they must take into account the specific cause of the stress and the level of control the individual has over the situation.

Emotion-focused coping, also called palliative coping, focuses on moderating and dealing with a person's emotional response. This palliative coping can take many healthy forms: exercise, yoga, mediation, and communication with support systems. Exercise is an especially potent form of coping, as regular exercise has been found to be just as effective at combating depression as prescription antidepressants.*1

Unfortunately, many students engage in counterproductive palliative coping as well: distraction through television, isolation and escape, and alcohol and drug abuse. These forms of coping create additional problems and ultimately contribute to, rather than lessen, stressors.

Problem-focused coping, also called instrumental coping, encompasses strategies that target the cause of the stress. This instrumental coping takes a form that targets the original cause. For example, if the cause of the stress is a class that is proving especially difficult, an instrumental coping strategy could include cutting back on your work hours and spending more time studying.

Unfortunately, many freshmen lack the ability in transitioning between palliative and instrumental coping; while palliative coping helps you manage your stress response, it does nothing to help you address the cause of that stress. Thus, it is essential that you use a balance of both palliative and instrumental coping strategies throughout your life.*2

*1 Babyak & Blumenthal, et al. "Exercise Treatment for Major Depression: Maintenance of Therapeutic Benefit at 10 Months." *Psychosomatic Medicine,* Sept/Oct 2000.

CSUB Student Health Center

The Student Health Service is open Monday through Friday 8:30 am to 5:00 pm of each regularly scheduled school day. The appointment desk is available daily at 8:00 am. A nurse is available during the lunch hour. Patient care for continuing students is available during quarter breaks and summer, dependent on staff availability.

The Student Health Service provides care on both an appointment and walk-in basis. Appointments are highly encouraged and help to limit student waiting time.

The Health Center is equipped with examining and treatment rooms, minor procedure rooms, x-ray, clinical laboratory and pharmacy services plus a willing, knowledgeable staff interested in serving students.

Who's Eligible?

All students currently enrolled for classes are eligible for care at the Health Center. The Runner Card or other photo ID card must be shown at the time of each visit. Students enrolled through the "Extended University" are eligible but must pay the $70 student health fee in the Accounting Office before the first visit for each quarter. "Extended University" students must show their current CSUB ID card or registration receipt at the time of each visit.

Oscar W. Rico, MD, Director/Physician

Basic Services

The SHS provides basic outpatient medical services for the diagnosis and treatment of acute and subacute conditions, illnesses and injuries. The medical staff is available for routine health care, women's services, minor surgery and urgent care including basic x-rays, laboratory and pharmacy. Student fees support the facility and provide many basic services, which are available at little or no cost. These include:

- Medical evaluation and counseling for individual health problems
- Laboratory tests needed to evaluate many acute problems
- X-rays needed for skeletal injuries
- Contraception and family planning counseling
- Programs in health education
- Anonymous or confidential HIV testing
- Emergency first aid for injuries on campus

For those services not covered by the mandatory health fee a charge is assessed based on the cost to provide the service. Generally, the cost at the SHS is far lower than the charges assessed off campus. Those augmented services for which there is a fee include:

- Medications
- Physical examinations
- Pap smears
- STD Testing
- Immunizations
- Lab or x-rays required for a class
- Any lab tests sent off campus
- Extended University Students
- Summer visits
- A variety of special lab tests can be done through the Health Center laboratory at a reasonable charge. Such lab specimens are sent to private, off campus laboratory facilities. The student is expected to pay in full at the time of specimen collection.

Complete fee schedule for augmented services are posted on the Health Center website and in the center itself. Students pay at the time of service with either cash or Runner Bucks.

Because of the nature of health care, medical records contain sensitive, privileged information about individuals and their medical information. Other than members of the Health Center staff directly involved in the care of an individual patient, no one may read or receive a copy of any part of a patient's record without the written permission of the patient (except as required by law). No member of the University's management, faculty or staff is entitled to information from any student's medical record without the student's written consent.

Health Center   (661) 654-2394
Health Center Fax (661) 654-3301
Pharmacy   (661) 654-3304

Services Not Provided

The Student Health Center does not provide emergency services of any kind. In addition, it is not the intention of the University or the SHS to provide comprehensive medical care for major problems or long term care of chronic/established medical conditions. Care is not provided for treatment of major illnesses, injuries or accidents that require either hospitalization or long term follow-up. Medical services in this category become the responsibility of the student. No off campus medical visits will be made by Health Center personnel at any time.

There are no after hours care or on-call services available at the CSUB Student Health Service, nor does the Health Center staff provide in-patient hospitalization services. Students should seek after hours and/or emergency care through their private physician or at a local hospital emergency room or urgent care center. All off campus medical care must be obtained at the student's expense.

CSUB Counseling Center

You will find all kinds of counseling and counselors at the University. At the Counseling Center, "counsel" is devoted to a particular set of needs: to clarify or understand feelings, alternatives, dilemmas, problems, questions, or crises. The need to be listened to or to sort out what is troubling you are issues that are actively addressed by the Counseling Center counselors.

The counselors are concerned with questions of work, study, career, and through all of these, your relationships to others, yourself and life. Students and counselors share a common interest: to help you, the student, make the most of your college experience by assisting you to:

- Think through and identify possible solutions to personal and social difficulties interfering with your educational experience;

- Develop a better understanding of yourself;

- Plan your longer-term educational and life goals;

- Gain a better understanding of your feelings, attitudes, motivations, interests, abilities, strengths, and weaknesses;

- Develop self-improvement skills;

- Understand the reasons for your learning problems;

- Cope with any stresses or crisis situations that leave you unsure of where to turn or what to do;

- Adjust to the many factors involved in living as a student;

- Develop satisfying personal relationships.

Who's Eligible?

All the services of the Counseling Center are available to all students who are enrolled in the regular University. These services are voluntary and covered by registration fees. Students who are enrolled in the Extended University or Intensive English Language Center (IELC) are not eligible for services and are encouraged to check Community Resources for appropriate mental health services.

Counseling Services

The University provides services to address the mental health needs of college students at the Counseling Center and to help students develop their maximum potential while pursuing their educational and personal goals, as well as to help remove any emotional or psychological barriers that may interfere with students' successful graduation from CSUB.

Professional counseling services are provided to all registered CSUB students at the Counseling Center. Outreach, consultation, and emergency response services are also provided to students, faculty, and staff.

The licensed, professional, and caring counselors who staff the Counseling Center provide, free of charge, confidential individual and group services in the following areas:

- **Crisis Intervention** - Counselors are available at all times that the Center is open to provide crisis intervention assistance.

- **Educational Counseling** - Educational counseling includes selecting an appropriate major, working on academic problems, and educational planning. Counselors provide opportunities for identifying interests, goals, and skills, and learning decision-making skills.

- **General Studies Courses** - Each quarter a variety of General Studies courses are offered. Courses are typically available in such areas as self-esteem, stress management, parenting, test anxiety, and adult children from dysfunctional families.

- **Personal Counseling** - Personal counseling is an opportunity to meet on a one-to-one basis with a licensed counselor to explore various needs and concerns. Concerns include relationships, abuse, and emotional issues such as loneliness, self-confidence, anger, and depression. Personal counseling may address any issue which influences a person's sense of well-being and progress in school. Due to high demands for services, an appointment may be necessary and the number of individual counseling sessions is limited.

661-654-3366

http://www.csub.edu/counselingcenter

When Students Should Seek Counseling

Students commonly seek counseling when they encounter a level of distress, which they feel unable to handle alone. In the past, students have most commonly sought counseling services at CSUB Counseling Center to address the following kinds of issues:

- Anger
- Depression, apathy, low energy, poor motivation
- Anxiety, persistent worry, panic attacks
- Relationship issues, difficulties with intimacy, abusive relationships
- Sexual problems/dysfunction
- Family issues
- Low self-esteem
- Sexual abuse or assault
- Eating disorder, episodic binge-eating, restricted intake
- Loneliness
- Sleep disturbances

Counseling Center Staff

Students typically try to work with these issues alone for a while before getting assistance. By seeking the assistance of a professional counselor, students can find non-judgmental acceptance and a level of expertise and objectivity that others who are closer to you (e.g. family or friends or even faculty) may not be able to provide.

Although recent studies have shown that 25-30% of college students report significant signs of depression, 58% of those students who sought help from the campus counseling center reported that counseling helped them stay in school and 61% reported that counseling helped with their academic performance.*

Most students report a significant improvement in functioning within just a few sessions with a professional counselor. For others, a positive experience with short-term counseling provides them with the confidence to pursue other sources of support such as group therapy, support group attendance, or more open ended individual or family counseling with a therapist in the community.

Because some presenting issues require further attention and time than is realistically available within the short-term counseling model, the counselor may determine that a referral to a more appropriate treatment setting or provider in the community is indicated. Should this be the case for you, your counselor will work closely with you to identify the most appropriate referrals given your circumstance, personal resources, and individual needs.

*"Mental Health: A College Issue." *NEA Advoc*ate. 26.6 (June 2009). 3.

Habits and Addictions

While many students see college as the time to experiment with alcohol and drugs as both recreation and, as previously discussed, palliative-coping strategies, there are consequences to this behavior.

Caffeine is the preeminent drug of choice for college students. Whether it is a *venti café latté,* an energy drink, or No-Doze, students turn to caffeine as a pick-me-up in the mornings and as a drink to stay awake during late night study sessions. In moderation, caffeine can reduce drowsiness and increase energy levels. However, caffeine also causes dehydration, can provoke anxiety and tremors, can interfere will sleep, and can aggravate heart conditions and high blood pressure. Furthermore, caffeine is addictive, and withdrawal symptoms include severe headaches and fatigue.

While tobacco is another legal drug, its effects are more severe: emphysema, heart disease, and lung cancer. Smoking can also exacerbate allergies and asthma, and considering that Kern County's air quality already ranks among the worst in the nation, smoking may not be the wisest of choices.

At some point in your college life, you may be faced with illegal drugs (if you haven't already). These include marijuana, cocaine, heroin, amphetamines, and crystal meth. These drugs are so addictive because they stimulate the brain's pleasure centers; the consequence of addiction is that these same centers become immune to any source of pleasure other than the drug to which the person has become addicted. Besides the threat of overdose and addiction, there is also the possibility of being arrested and incarcerated.

Illegal drugs are not the only artificial stimulant of the brain's pleasure center; prescription drugs fill the same role: Xanax, Vicodin, Lorcet, Lortab, OxyContin, Percocet, Percodan, Dexedrine, Ativan, Valium, Desoxyn. As with the illegal drugs, these carry the risks of overdose and addiction.

However, the drug of the greatest concern to college students is alcohol.

Facts about College Drinking

Death: 1,700 college students between the ages of 18 and 24 die each year from alcohol-related unintentional injuries, including motor vehicle crashes.

Injury: 599,000 students between the ages of 18 and 24 are unintentionally injured under the influence of alcohol.

Assault: More than 696,000 students between the ages of 18 and 24 are assaulted by another student who has been drinking.

Sexual Abuse: More than 97,000 students between the ages of 18 and 24 are victims of alcohol-related sexual assault or date rape.

Unsafe Sex: 400,000 students between the ages of 18 and 24 had unprotected sex and more than 100,000 students between the ages of 18 and 24 report having been too intoxicated to know if they consented to having sex.

Academic Problems: About 25 percent of college students report academic consequences of their drinking including missing class, falling behind, doing poorly on exams or papers, and receiving lower grades overall.

Health Problems/Suicide Attempts: More than 150,000 students develop an alcohol-related health problem and between 1.2 and 1.5 percent of students indicate that they tried to commit suicide within the past year due to drinking or drug use.

Drunk Driving: 2.1 million students between the ages of 18 and 24 drove under the influence of alcohol last year.

Alcohol Abuse and Dependence: 31 percent of college students met criteria for a diagnosis of alcohol abuse and 6 percent for a diagnosis of alcohol dependence in the past 12 months, according to questionnaire-based self-reports about their drinking.*

*National Institute on Alcohol Abuse and Alcoholism. 2007 www.collegedrinkingprevention.gov

Sexuality

While sex is a natural human drive and can take a relationship to a new level of emotional and physical intimacy, sexual behavior carries with it emotional issues of self-confidence, self-respect, and self-esteem. Therefore, it is essential that you remain true to yourself as you choose to engage in whatever level of sexual behavior you feel is right for you.

As with any relationship, it is essential that you listen to your feelings. Don't let someone else pressure you into a sexual relationship. If you feel hesitation before sex, guilt afterward, or a lack of desire at any point during intercourse, discuss those feelings with your partner.

Be sure to practice safe sex. While no birth control method is 100% effective, condoms are 90% effective and will reduce the chance of contracting STDs as well.

The key to an effective intimate relationship is healthy communication. Be open with your expectations, and don't expect your partner will be able to read your mind or will know what you want or don't want. Be assertive with your emotional and physical standards, and expect your partner to be just as open with you. Likewise, be sure to ask questions of your partner. If your partner hasn't made his or her expectations known, ask him or her what those expectations are.

Along with communication comes respect. Respect your partner's choices even if those choices aren't the same as your own. Healthy relationships are build on communication, respect, and trust. If you can't trust your partner to respect what you communicate to him or her, then that is a relationship not worth continuing.

Remember to stand your ground. This is your life, and it is yours to control, so don't let someone else dominate your goals and needs. An effective relationship is a partnership in which each side respects the other.

Sexually Transmitted Diseases

According to studies, 25% of college students will develop a sexually transmitted disease, and of the 19 million new infections that occur each year, half of them are among young people ages 15-24.*

Why is this such a concern?

Even if treated early, STDs are a major health risk and can have devastating effects on your life: damage to the reproductive organs, infertility, cancer, and death. Unfortunately, rates of infection of four major STDs — Chlamydia, gonorrhea, syphilis, and herpes—have been increasing, and half of all new HIV infections occur in people 25 years of age or younger.

To avoid contracting an STD, you should follow these guidelines:

- Know your partner; it takes time to develop a healthy relationship.

- Don't assume your partner is healthy just because he or she looks healthy. The most common symptom of an STD is the lack of any symptom.

- Latex condoms and dental dams can offer some protection against STDs, but the only totally effective method of preventing an infection is abstinence.

If you think you may have contracted an STD, contact the Health Center immediately so that you may get tested and start a treatment program if needed. As with all illnesses, early detection is the key to effective treatment.

CSUB Health Center: (661) 654-2394

* Weinstock H, et al. "Sexually Transmitted Diseases among American Youth: Incidence and Prevalence Estimates, 2000." *Perspectives on Sexual and Reproductive Health* 2004; 36.1.

Sexual Violence

It is a troubling fact that 20% to 25% of women in college reported experiencing an attempted or completed rape in college.*1

The image most people have of a rapist is a shadowy figure lurking in the bushes waiting to pounce on an unwitting stranger.

The reality is much different.

In fact, stranger rape is much rarer than acquaintance rape: 90% of college women who are victims or rape or attempted rape knew their assailant, who was usually a classmate, friend, boyfriend, ex-boyfriend, or other acquaintance.*2

*1 Fisher BS, Cullen FT, Turner MG. 2000. The sexual victimization of college women. Washington: Department of Justice (US), National Institute of Justice; Publication No. NCJ 182369.

*2 United States. Department of Justice. Office of Community Oriented Policing Services. Acquaintance Rape of College Students. By Rana Simpson. Problem Oriented Guides for Police. Problem Specific Guide Series. No 17.

Your Right to Know

Q: I'd be interested in getting information on crime on our campus. How can I do that?

A: The CSUB Police Department provides crime statistics information for the most recent three year period. Additionally, the department maintains a daily log of offenses committed on our campus. You can obtain a copy of "Your Right to Know" booklet at our department. The daily log is also available for public review. The Public Safety/University Police web page is on-line and will have information on all our programs, campus crime data, and other useful information. Log on to www.csub.edu, then click on the Public Safety link.

When Calling the University Police (654-2111) or 911 . . .

• Give your name

• Describe the condition clearly and accurately

• Give your telephone number or extension number

• Give building and room number or other specific location

• DON'T HANG UP! Let the person to whom you are talking end the conversation; other information may be needed.

CSUB Sexual Assault Policy

If a victim reports a sexual assault to someone on campus other than the University Police, that person should encourage the victim to contact the University Police. The University Police will see that the victim receives medical assistance, information on legal rights and options (including criminal prosecution, civil prosecution, Victim's Assistance aid, the disciplinary process through the university, and the availability of mediation), as well as contact any family member or friend upon request by the victim. If the victim has been assaulted off-campus, the University Police will assist the victim in contacting the appropriate police agency.

First aid and urgent care is available at the Student Health Center. Individuals needing full medical evaluation, including evidence collection, will be referred and transported to a local emergency care hospital by the University Police. Evidence collection and documentation of the incident are of critical importance in prosecution of the assailant.

A written crime alert bulletin will be issued by the University Police to the campus community as soon as possible. Those details of the assault that are essential to the health and safety of the campus community shall be released. The protection of the identity of the victim will be of the highest priority.

Counseling services are available through either Health Programs and Psychological Counseling or Student Development.

In an effort to promote awareness of rape, acquaintance rape, and other sex offenses, a number of campus offices (University Police, Health Programs and Psychological Counseling, Student Development, and Housing) offer crime prevention classes at various times during the academic year. Consult these departments for schedules.

University Police: 654-2111.

Q: I'm here at night, and while I try to walk with friends, sometimes that's not possible. I feel uncomfortable walking to my car at night. Do you provide escorts?

A: Yes. We provide a 24 hour escort service. Call our department at Ext. 2111 and we'll have an officer or Campus Service Officer escort you to your car, dorm or other location on campus.

Rape Aggression Defense (R.A.D.) (http://www.csub.edu/BAS/police/rad.shtml)

Once a year, usually in the spring quarter, the CSUB Police Department offers a two-day class on the Rape Aggression Defense System, which is the largest women's self-defense training program in the country, being taught by more than 350 universities and municipal law enforcement departments nationwide.

The Rape Aggression Defense System is a program of realistic, self-defense tactics and techniques. The RAD system is a comprehensive course for women that begins with awareness, prevention, risk reduction and avoidance, while progressing on to the basics of hands-on defense training.

This 12 hour class is free of charge to everyone on campus.

For more information, contact the CSUB Police Department at 654-2111.

More Friendly Faces

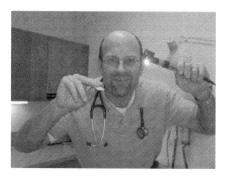

Christopher Gambrioli, M.D.
.Physician

Putting Skills to Work: Staying in College

1. Get into groups of three to five students.

2. Choose one of the four clusters that lead to students dropping out: adjustment, difficulty, incongruence, or isolation.

3. Brainstorm, discuss, and evaluate various palliative and problem-focused coping strategies that would help a student overcome that cluster.

4. Prepare a presentation for the rest of the class that presents the best (and worst) of these strategies to class.

5. After you give the presentation, discuss what you did well and what you could improve next time.

Kelsey Bailey, R.N., Registered Nurse

Putting Skills to Work: Physical Health

1. Get into groups of three to five students.

2. Choose a location on or near campus where a student can exercise or eat a healthy meal. Research the specific details of that location. This research could include photographs.

3. Prepare a presentation for the rest of the class that describes and advocates this location.

4. After you give the presentation, discuss what you did well and what you could improve next time.

Putting Skills to Work: Emotional Health

1. Get into groups of three to five students.

2. Assume that a CSUB student is experiencing stress from school, work, and / or relationships. Besides going to the Counseling Center, what else can a student do at CSUB to help him or her deal with this stress? Choose a location on or near campus where a student can ease this emotional stress. Research the specific details of that location; this research could include photographs.

3. Prepare a presentation for the rest of the class that describes and advocates this location.

4. After you give the presentation, discuss what you did well and what you could improve next time.

Chapter Four: Advising and Registration

The Student Success and Retention Center (http://www.csub.edu/ssrc/)

The advising and registration process can be overwhelming for many students. The process used to be much different. In the 1980s, students had assigned times when they could walk through registration in DDH. Each student went to the table with the class he or she needed. Students signed their names on the class list, and that was it. The process is now multi-faceted. Often, students do not understand how the process works, and this results in confusion and fear. There are really just two steps to our current process. First, you meet with your advisor to decide which classes you need. Second, you register online.

The vision of the (Student Success & Retention Center) SSRC is to achieve excellence in academic advising by being the central location for retention-based academic advising at CSUB and promoting achievement of our student's academic and life goals. The SSRC is located in the Administration East Building (AE 100), between Title V/Oasis Center and the Art Department. The mission of the SSRC is to provide a place where

- Students develop a partnership with a core set of professional faculty and staff advisors, empowering them to set and achieve goals as well as discover their individual potential.

- Students receive the most up-to-date and accurate information for their plan of study, leading to an efficient path toward graduation.

- Advising is viewed as a teaching tool and learning process not just a service provided to the student.

- Advisors honor the unique nature and interests of each student. Advising is shaped to fit the diverse needs of our student population.

Registration Procedures

Course registration occurs after a student has been properly and formally admitted into the university and/or is a continuing student. Before a student attempts to register, it is strongly suggested that he/she should have:

- Spoken with an academic advisor;
- Cleared all holds and obligations to the university;
- Taken any necessary tests or prerequisites;
- Obtained proper registration appointment time disbursed by the registration office via e-mail;
- Obtained a University Catalog and Schedule of Classes.

In addition, students should become aware of and responsible for all academic policies and procedures as outlined in the University Catalog and Schedule of Classes.

Finding Your Advisor

You will have to meet with your advisor before registering for next quarter's classes. To find out who your advisor is, fill out the form on the following website.

http://www.csub.edu/ssrc/advisor.shtml

Then, go to the department and sign up for advising with your specific advisor.

Maintaining Your Records

In order to fulfill your responsibility for planning your education, you should assemble and maintain an academic portfolio (which should always be taken to every advising appointment) containing the following kinds of information:

• A list of courses taken to show progress toward your objectives.

• Transcripts from all schools and CSUB's evaluation of transfer credit if you are an undergraduate transfer student.

• CSU, Bakersfield grades (available online.)

• Test Results from entrance exams, English proficiency, Math proficiency or placement exams, and advanced placement exams.

• Copies of important communications to and from the University.

• A copy of your class schedule once you have registered for courses.

Meeting the Requirements

It is important you are cognizant of the graduation requirements. You do not want to be in your "final" quarter and discover that you still need to take the Graduation Writing Assessment Requirement and have to come back for one more class. Likewise, you probably do not want to take two classes that fulfill the same requirement. Keeping track of these requirements and your progress in meeting them will enable you to smoothly work your way to graduation and will allow you to more easily navigate any bumps in the road. The next four pages comprise various worksheets designed to assist you in planning your course schedules so that they include these requirements.

One important thing to remember is that these classes are not offered every quarter, so you will want to review the course schedules to see which classes are being offered when. Some courses are offered every quarter, some courses are offered once a year, and some courses are offered once every two or three years. As such, it is best to have back-up plans in case the class you want to take is full or is not being offered.

These forms will help you navigate your General Education requirements. For the requirements specific to your major or minor, speak to the advisor for that department, or check the department's webpage.

Holds

Occasionally, you may have a hold you will need to clear before you can register for classes. Maybe you never got your immunizations, or maybe you "forgot" to pay your tuition.

You can review your holds from the Holds section of myCSUB. The details link opens the Your Holds page, which provides additional information regarding holds placed on services, enrollment, financial aid, and accounting. The Item List shows the Hold Item, Amount, Currency, Institution, Term, and Department associated with the Hold. You can determine how and by when to resolve your holds by clicking the Hold Item., which will allow you to view information about a specific hold and determine whom to contact and how to resolve it. The Hold Item page is separated into two sections: Reason and Contact and Instructions. The Reason and Contact section shows the institution, term, reason for the hold, department placing the hold, and the contact person, and the Instructions section will display any applicable instructions.

General Education & Other Graduation Requirements Worksheet

Catalog Year:

UNITS

      RESIDENT (45): _____   GENERAL EDUCATION (72): _____

      UPPER DIVISION (60): _____   TOTAL (180): _____

GENERAL EDUCATION (1997 and subsequent catalogs)

PART 1: Lower Division Component

A. Communication in the English Language   C. Arts and Humanities (3 of 5)

      A1: _____   C1: _____

      A2: _____   C2: _____

      A3: _____   C3: _____

      C4: _____

      C5: _____

B. Mathematics, Life and Physical   D. Social and Behavioral Sciences

   Sciences (B3 is lab requirement)   (3 of 5)

      B1: _____   D1: _____

      B2: _____   D2: _____

      B3: _____   D3: _____

      B4: _____   D4: _____

      D5: _____

PART 2: Upper Division Component

Theme 1: _____ Theme 2: _____ Theme 3: _____

OTHER GRADUATION REQUIREMENTS

AMERICAN INSTITUTIONS REQUIREMENT

1. U.S. HISTORY: _____ 2. STATE/LOCAL GOVERNMENT: _____

CSUB 101 RR RUSH-A SEM. REQUIREMENT: _____

GENDER RACE AND ETHNICITY REQUIREMENT: _____

GRADUATION WRITING ASSESSMENT REQUIREMENT (GWAR):   _____

FOREIGN LANGUAGE: _____

(Two years of high school foreign language or foreign course at the 101 level or higher)

Area A: Communication in the English Language
One course from each sub-area.

A1. Speaking and listening
Comm 108
Thtr 232

A2. Writing and reading
Engl 110

A3. Writing-intensive critical thinking and logical reasoning
Anth 120
Anth 121
Phil 102
Soc 120

General Education
and Other Graduation Requirements
(revised May 20, 2011)

You may access this file electronically from "Course Schedules," which provides this list as well as a list highlighting the GE classes offered during the current quarter.

Note: Students must earn a C or higher in Areas A1, A2, A3, and B4 in order to meet the General Education Requirement.

Area B: Mathematics, Life and Physical Sciences - *(See Note**)*
One course from each sub-area.

B1. Physical Sciences
Chem 100A
Chem 100B
Chem 100C
Chem 100D
Chem 100 E (effective Winter 2011)
Geol 100
Geol 110
Geol 120
Geol 201
Geol 205
Phys 110

B2. Life Sciences
Biol 100
Biol 103

B3. Science laboratory related to either B1 or B2
Science labs are included in the above courses.

B4. Mathematics
Math 101
Math 140
Psyc 200

Area C: Arts and Humanities

One course from three of the following sub-areas

C1. Art or Performing Arts

Art 101

Art 201

Art 202

Mus 101

Mus 105

Mus 295

Thtr 101

Thtr 273

C2. Foreign Languages (103 level or above fluency courses)

Fren 102 (effective Winter 2011)

Fren 103

Fren 201

Fren 202

Span 102 (effective Winter 2011)

Span 103

Span 105

Span 201

Span 202

Span 210

C3. History

Hist 102

Hist 202

Hist 204

Hist 206

Hist 210

Hist 211

Hist 212

Hist 222

Hist 240

Hist 250

C4. Literature

Engl 101

Engl 205

Engl 207

Engl 208

Engl 235

Engl 272

Engl 290

Engl 294

Engl 295

C5. Philosophy/Religious Studies

Phil 100

Phil 101

RS 100

RS 110

RS 111

Area D: Social and Behavioral Sciences

One course from three of the following sub-areas

D1. Anthropology

Anth 100

Anth 104

Anth 106

Anth 250

Anth 251

Anth 253

D2. Economics

Econ 100

Econ 105

Econ 201

Econ 202

D3. Political Sciences

PlSi 101

PlSi 102

PPA 275 (effective Winter 2011)

D4. Psychology

Psyc 100

D5. Sociology

Soc 100

SW 200

Upper Division Themes: One course in each Theme is required.

Students must have junior standing (90 or more units) before taking Theme courses.

Theme 1: Natural Sciences and Technology
InSt 312*
Sci 351A
Sci 351B
Sci 351C
Sci 352A
Sci 352B
Sci 352C
Sci 353
Sci 354A
Sci 354B
Sci 355A
Sci 355B
Sci 355C
Sci 355D
Sci 355E

Theme 2: Arts and Humanities	
Art 382	Mus 380
Art 384	Mus 390
Art 483	Mus 395
Comm 345	Phil 302
Comm 378	Phil 308
Comm 407	Phil 310
Comm 460	Phil 316
Engl 362	Phil/PlSi 333
Engl 363	Phil/RS 342
Engl 365	Phil/RS 363
Engl 366	RS 313
Engl 373	RS 316
Engl 395	RS 320
Engl 414	RS 323
Engl 475	RS 336
Fren 301	RS 378
Fren 302	RS 465
Fren 380	Span 301
Hist 303	Span 302
Hist 309	Span 303
Hist 325	Span 416
Hist 401	Span 419
Hist 426	Span 427
Hist 443	Span 428
Hist 445	Thtr 371
Hist 453	Thtr 372
InSt 312*	Thtr 379
	Thtr 385

Theme 3: Social and Behavioral Science
Anth 330
Anth 340
Anth 350
Anth 351
Anth 370
Anth 475
BA 374
BehS 307
BehS 382
CrJu 310
CrJu 340
CrJu 380
CrJu 494
Econ 305
Econ 310
Econ 311
Econ 370
Econ 410
PLSI 304
PLSI 308
PLSI 322
PLSI 328
PLSI 332
PPA 300
PPA 340
Psyc 312
Psyc 332
Psyc 435
Soc 312
Soc 339
Soc 350
Soc 352
Soc 405
Soc 450

General Education and Other Graduation Requirements

* May count for only one theme

Other Graduation Requirements

Gender, Race, Ethnicity
(One course)

Anth 252	Hist 421
Anth 339	Hist 462
Anth 438	Hist 465
BA 200	Hist 466
BehS 435	Hist 467
CAFS 320	Hist 468
Comm 360	InSt 205
Comm 370	Nurs 327
CrJu 325	PEAK 430
CrJu 330	Phil 381
CrJu 345	Phil 382
CrJu 430	PlSi 329
Econ 380	PlSi 339
Econ 381	Psyc 340
EDBI 475	Psyc 421
EDTE 416 (effective Winter 2011)	Psyc 442
Engl 364	RS 326
Engl 370	RS 360
Engl 374	Soc 327
Engl 420	Soc 335
Fren 425	Soc 336
Fren 426	Soc 337
	Soc 338
	Soc 370
	Span 425
	Thtr 381
	Thtr 383

General Education and Other Graduation Requirements

Graduation Writing Assessment Requirement (GWAR)
(must have junior standing, 90 or more units, prior to completing course or test)

Admin 510
Comm 304
Comm 306
Comm 311
Engl 305
Engl 310
Engl 311
Hist 300
PPA 493 (effective Winter 2011)

Students must earn a C or higher to meet this requirement and may also test out of the GWAR course by scoring an 8 or higher on the Graduation Writing Exam.

State and Local Government *(One course)*

PlSi 101
PPA 275 (effective Winter 2011)

US History Requirement
(One course)

Hist 231
Hist 232

Freshman Orientation

CSUB 101

Foreign Language Requirement

Two years of high school or one college quarter/semester

California State University Bakersfield

FRESHMAN YEAR

Fall	Winter	Spring
_____ ( )	_____ ( )	_____ ( )
_____ ( )	_____ ( )	_____ ( )
_____ ( )	_____ ( )	_____ ( )
_____ ( )	_____ ( )	_____ ( )
_____ ( )	_____ ( )	
_____ ( )	_____ ( )	
_____ ( )	_____ ( )	

Total Credits ____

SOPHOMORE YEAR

Fall	Winter	Spring
_____ ( )	_____ ( )	_____ ( )
_____ ( )	_____ ( )	_____ ( )
_____ ( )	_____ ( )	_____ ( )
_____ ( )	_____ ( )	_____ ( )
_____ ( )	_____ ( )	
_____ ( )	_____ ( )	
_____ ( )	_____ ( )	

Total Credits ____

JUNIOR YEAR

Fall	Winter	Spring
_____ ( )	_____ ( )	_____ ( )
_____ ( )	_____ ( )	_____ ( )
_____ ( )	_____ ( )	_____ ( )
_____ ( )	_____ ( )	_____ ( )
_____ ( )	_____ ( )	
_____ ( )	_____ ( )	
_____ ( )	_____ ( )	

Total Credits ____

SENIOR YEAR

Fall	Winter	Spring
_____ ( )	_____ ( )	_____ ( )
_____ ( )	_____ ( )	_____ ( )
_____ ( )	_____ ( )	_____ ( )
_____ ( )	_____ ( )	_____ ( )
_____ ( )	_____ ( )	
_____ ( )	_____ ( )	
_____ ( )	_____ ( )	

Total Credits ____

Total Credits ☐

Choosing Your Electives

A liberal education is one in which a student is exposed to many diverse fields and ways of thinking. Rather than being trained in one specific field, the student sees the bigger picture, the world in which all the fields interact. More specifically, the CSU system has formulated its rationale for General Education Requirements as follows:

- *develop and reinforce basic skills in writing, speaking, and listening in the English language, in critical thinking and logical reasoning, and in quantitative reasoning;*

- *provide students with a breadth of exposure to mathematics, life and physical sciences, arts and humanities, and social and behavioral sciences;*

- *provide students with an in-depth exposure to themes of importance in the modern world-natural science and technology, arts and humanities, and social and behavioral sciences;*

- *assist students in the process of becoming well-informed and responsible citizens;*

- *increase students' understanding of human diversity and their tolerance for differences of perceptions, ideas and values;*

- *give students an international and multicultural perspective on issues and problems confronting human society and the natural world; and*

- *facilitate the process of ethical development and responsibility at the personal, interpersonal, and societal levels.*

Given the reasons for the general education classes overall, how should you decide which specific courses to take?

- Follow your interests. Studies have shown that students learn more when the course material matches their personal interests, so you will probably be more successful in a class that already interests you.

- Use a class to explore a major. If you're thinking about majoring in Sociology, take a sociology class to see if the major is a good fit for you.

- Use a class to address your weaknesses. If you know that you have a gap in your knowledge when it comes to one part of the world, take a class that focuses on that area.

- Use a class to build your resume. If you know you want to work in a certain part of the world, take classes that will further your knowledge of that culture.

Class Level

Unlike in high school, your class level does not reflect how many years you have been at the institution. For example, a student could spend three years at a college and still be considered a freshmen. Rather, class level depends on the number of units a student has successfully completed.

Freshmen	44.5 or fewer quarter units
Sophomore	45 to 89.5 quarter units
Junior	90 to 134.5 quarter units
Senior	135 or more quarter units
Post-Baccaluareate	Possesses acceptable baccalaureate or advanced degree; may be admitted to a credential or certificate program, but is not admitted to a graduate degree curriculum.
Graduate	Formally admitted to a graduate degree curriculum

It is important to maintain your GPA, for this is how many people will judge your college experience. Unlike your transcripts, which indicate your knowledge in given areas, your GPA reflects your diligence and work ethic overall, which is why it is of so much importance to graduate schools and employers. A solid GPA signifies that you are hard-working and dependable, two valuable qualities.

Most of the grade symbols are identical to those in high school or other colleges, but there are two categories that may be unfamiliar to you. A W indicates that a student dropped the course after the third week of class. While this letter is on the transcripts, it does not factor into GPA. A WU, on the other hand, indicates that a student stopped coming to class but never officially dropped. Furthermore, a WU translates into an F for GPA purposes and affects Financial Aid, so it is essential that you officially withdraw from a class if you need to drop it.

Grade Symbol	Explanation	Grade Points
A	Excellent	4.0
A-	-	3.7
B+	-	3.3
B	Good	3.0
B-	-	2.7
C+	-	2.3
C	Average	2.0
C-	-	1.7
D+	-	1.3
D	Passing	1.0
D-	-	0.7
F	Failing	0
W	Withdraw	0
I	Incomplete	0
CR	Credit	0
NC	No-Credit	0
RD	Report Delayed	0
SP	Satisfactory Progress	0
WU	Unauthorized Withdrawal	0

Grades

W (Withdraw) – This symbol indicates that the student was permitted to drop the course after the third full week of classes. A course with a "W" grade is not counted as work attempted. It carries no connotation of quality of student's performance and is not used in calculating grade point average or progress points.

Withdrawals after the third week of classes and prior to the last three weeks of classes are permissible only for serious and compelling reasons. Permission to withdraw during this period is granted only with the approval of the instructor and the department chairman or school dean. All requests for permission to withdraw during this period and all approvals must be made in writing in prescribed forms that state the reasons for the withdrawal. Withdrawals are not permitted during the final three weeks of instruction except in cases such as accident or serious illness, where the cause of withdrawal is clearly beyond the student's control and the assignment of an "Incomplete" is not practical. Most withdrawals in this time period involve total withdrawal from the campus and must be endorsed by the dean of students.

WU (Unauthorized Withdrawal) – The symbol "WU" indicates that an enrolled student did not withdraw from the course but failed to complete course requirements. It is used when, in the opinion of the instructor, completed assignments or course activities or both were insufficient to make normal evaluation of academic performance possible. For purposes of grade point average and progress point computation, this symbol is equivalent to an "F."

Frequently Asked Questions

- I need to update my address and contact information. To whom do I send it?

  You may update your information through MyCSUB.

- I've registered for classes. What happens next?

  You will not receive a billing statement in the mail. Billing notices are sent via email. It is imperative that the campus also has current address and contact information on file.

- The class I want to register is closed. What should I do?

  If the course you are registering for is full, try selecting another section for the same course. You may also use the waitlist function in MyCSUB, but being on a waitlist does not guarantee your enrollment in the class. If an instructor allows students to add the course, you must obtain a signature on an "Add" slip. Submit the "Add" slip to the records office for processing.

- The class I want to register for overlaps in time with another course. Can I still take both courses?

  Yes. However, registration for courses with overlaps in time is not allowed online or by telephone. Speak to the records office staff member to complete your registration for this course. The student must be fully aware that the course times overlap, and it is the responsibility of the student to make arrangements with the instructor.

- When I registered for a course, it says I have a "prerequisite" error. What is this?

  If the registration system says you have a prerequisite problem with a specific course, you will have to go to the appropriate department to get an approval signature on an Add form. Take the signed form to the Records office for processing and registration of the course.

Add / Drop Form

The Add / Drop Form is what you will use for adding or dropping classes after on-line registration has ended; you can pick up copies of the form at the Office of Admissions and Records.

Be sure to give all the required information and collect the required signatures, and make sure to complete and submit the form yourself; your instructors will not return the forms for you.

Add / Drop Request Form
California State University, Bakersfield
Office of Admissions and Records
9001 Stockdale Highway | Bakersfield, CA | 93311-1022
(661) 654-3036 | Fax (661) 654-3389

Please Note:
-If you are dropping all courses after the 3rd week of classes, please fill out a Complete Withdrawal from Term request form.

-Department Chair's signature is required after the 3rd week of classes for dropping courses.

Last:_____ First:_____ M.I. _____ CSUB ID #:_____

Quarter: [ ] Fall [ ] Winter [ ] Spring [ ] Summer   Year:_____   Level: Undergraduate____ Graduate____

Course Request Number (CRN)	Course Department & Number	Section	Units	Check Add	Drop	Instructor's Name Printed	Approvals, instructor/department signatures, comments
TO BE COMPLETED BY THE STUDENT							

State reason for DROP (Required after the 3rd week of classes)

I am aware of the conditions of this add/drop transaction including any effects on my academic progress, records, and fees.

Student's Signature: _____ Date:_____

Total units before change
Total units after change

Office Use Only
By: ____ Date: ____

Financial Aid & Scholarships: www.csub.edu/finaid

In its simplest definition, financial aid is money that helps pay the cost of your education. The money comes from several sources. The federal or state governments, private donors, and University aid is available in the form of grants (awards that need not be repaid), loans (awards that must be repaid), work-study employment and/or scholarships. Students are encouraged to contact the OFA&S for specific application instructions, and/or visit the website for information on How to Apply – a General Overview of the Financial Aid Application & Delivery Process; Tips for Success; and simplified Checklists to assist with a smooth transition to CSUB.

Campus-based Aid

Campus-based Aid

The Financial Aid Office requires a Free Application for Federal Student Aid (FAFSA) be filed for the upcoming academic year beginning January 2 and no later than March 2 for priority consideration. Awards are contingent upon the availability of funds. Students applying after March 2 will be considered for financial aid only if funds are available.

Federal Pell Grant

Students may apply by completing the FAFSA.

How Need is Determined

When you apply for financial aid, your FAFSA is analyzed by the Federal Processor, and the results are forwarded to the Financial Aid Office at CSUB. On-time applicants should be notified by May 15 of their eligibility.

Scholarships

Applications for the upcoming academic year are available beginning February 1 and have a priority filing date of April 2. Applicants should have a minimum GPA of 3.0 for most scholarship programs.

Satisfactory Academic Progress

All financial aid is contingent upon admission to and enrollment at this campus, and on maintaining "satisfactory academic progress" toward a stated degree objective. The Satisfactory Academic Progress Policy statement is provided on the CSUB Office of Financial Aid & Scholarships web page at www.csub.edu/finaid/sap.shtml and is also available in the Financial Aid Office.

For additional financial aid information, contact the Office of Financial Aid and Scholarships or visit our web page at www.csub.edu/finaid.

William D. Ford Federal Direct Loan

Applicants are encouraged to complete a FAFSA for the upcoming academic year beginning January 2. Applicants must also complete a separate promissory note and loan entrance counseling requirement online.

Waiting Lists / Full Classes

HELP! The classes I want are full. What do I do?

This is a common problem, but it's one that has solutions, so here's what to do if the class you need is full:

1. Use MyCSUB's waitlist function to be added to the waitlist. The system will automatically add students from the waitlist to the class if any student drops the course.

2. Email the professor.

3. Attend the class. The email is worthless if you do not show up to class. In fact, trying to add is nearly impossible unless you are in class. The waiting list policy of the university states that you must be in class to remain on the waiting list. Furthermore, if you miss a class you are trying to add, you are sending the professor the signal that he or she is adding a student who already disregards class attendance.

4. If you have sent the email and gone to the class, you might also try the Department Secretary for the course you are trying to add. Often, the department secretaries have information on classes or professors who are willing to add students even if the class appears closed.

Dear Professor Cooper,

I am Belinda Carlisle, a first year student here at CSUB. Although your Psychology 101 course (CRN 23225) seems to be full, I was wondering if it would be possible to add. I promise to be a diligent student and an excellent addition to class. If it is not possible to add, would you be so kind as to add me to your waiting list. Thanks so much for considering this.

Sincerely, Belinda.

CSUB ID: 90012121

Waiting List Policy

On a waiting list, you are eligible for a place in the class

1. if you come to every class and

2. if you complete the work while you are there.

Being on a waiting list does not mean you are guaranteed a place in the class. It simply means you are welcome to wait for an opening in the class if you so desire. If no one drops out of the section you're attending, no students can add.

As a result, you should be aware of the last day to add and have a back-up choice if you need another class. This plan is especially important for financial aid recipients and for F-1 and J-1 visa holders, who must carry a full load to receive their financial aid. Being on a waiting list does not count as a class toward your full load.

Instructor-Initiated Drop Policy

If the class is full and has a waiting list, the professor has the right to have a student administratively dropped from class by the end of the second week of the term if the student has missed three consecutive class sessions and has not contacted the instructor. However, the student should not assume that he or she will be automatically dropped from this course due to non-attendance, so the student should complete a formal Drop Form if he or she wishes to withdraw from the course.

Building Life Skills: Note Taking

Taking notes is a vital college skill. When you are in class, your ability to listen actively to the speaker will greatly improve your retention of material. Taking good notes will help you listen actively and pay better attention in class.

- DO NOT try to write down every word your professor says. DO NOT fill every possible space on your page. Your notes should not be one long text but should have an organizational flow. Instead, you are looking for the key points from each lecture. When taking notes, you are paraphrasing, looking for the main ideas from the lecture.

- If your professor repeats or emphasizes information, that is a good indicator that the material is important. A good professor will be clear with his or her lectures, and if you're listening carefully, you'll be able to discern the information the professor thinks is most important.

- One way to test your notes is to take your notes to the professor's office to ask the professor if she or he thinks your notes are too detailed or too sparse. This will help you evaluate your note-taking skills.

Taking Notes

1. Leave blank space throughout your page. This will allow you to add subtopics or other information if your professor skips back to a point. Leaving blank space also makes reviewing your notes much easier.

2. Indent subtopics. You may want to learn the Cornell Note Taking System, but an equally valuable system is one that you may develop on your own: place major topics on the left hand side of the page, and place definitions, explanations, stories, formulas, and other information specific to those topics on the right hand side of the page.

3. Use boxes, arrows, circles, symbols, or any other visual cues to make your page of notes come to life.

4. Date each page and add the lecture topic to each page. This will make reviewing your notes and finding relevant information much easier.

5. Don't be afraid to ask the professor to stop and cover a key point again. One of the most important keys to your success at CSUB is for you to be an active student. Ask questions in class!

6. If you do not understand a point but do not feel comfortable asking for help at that moment, write a gigantic question mark with an arrow or some other symbol to indicate where your confusion began. Then, you can later ask for clarification of that point. Recognizing moments of confusion can be one of the most fruitful intellectual endeavors; they do not mean you are dumb, but they mean the opposite, since the greatest discoveries in all of human knowledge stemmed from moments of profound confusion!

7. Reread and review your readings after the lecture. If your professor added information or clarification to the reading, highlight or annotate the information the professor emphasized or elaborated. This will help when it comes time to studying for a test.

Reviewing Your Notes

Once you have learned to take good notes, you should get into the habit of reviewing class notes each day after class for five minutes and before the start of the next class. Some students take notes by hand and then copy then onto the computer. You should find your own best style, but note taking and note reviewing will certainly be a crucial part of your success at CSUB.

When you take serious lecture notes you're already processing the material through your memory banks and knowledge structure. In other words, by the end of the hour, you're already at least a quarter of the way toward where you want to be. And if you want to wring even more out of the experience, try writing your notes in complete sentences!

—Dr. John Maynard,
History Department

Creating Your Own Shorthand

When taking notes, remember that there are words that you use repeatedly throughout many different courses. One reason why shorthand is so important is that some professors tend to speak very quickly. Hence, you should develop your own system of shorthand. Here are some examples:

@=at

w/=with

w/o=without

♀=woman   ♀♀=women

♂=man   ♂♂=men

e.g.=for example.

Remember is to use your own symbols as you begin to write. For instance, I always used the letter p to signify pow-er. You may use the p to signify page. You may also abbreviate, so that in your psychology class Narcissistic Personality Disorder might become "Nar. Pers. Dis." But beware of abbreviating too much!

Chapter Five: Choosing Your Major

Many of you may already be facing pressure from your family and friends: "What are you going to major in?"

A major is a commitment of time and money, for you will be spending at least two years of your life buying books and studying for exams in your field of study. In other words, you do not necessarily want to rush into a major. Furthermore, a major is relatively meaningless for a freshmen; you probably will not start taking classes in your major until you are a sophomore or junior. Finally, only one in three college seniors graduate with a major in the same field they chose during their first year in college. In other words, take the time to find the major that is right for you, and do not feel bad if you change your mind.

The key to finding your major is to first find yourself. What kind of person are you? Do you enjoy working with others? Do you enjoy doing research?

To get a sense of who you are, answer these questions designed to help you reflect on your personal interests, abilities, and values.

Personal Interests

What tends to grab and keep your attention?

What sorts of things are you naturally curious about?

What are your favorite hobbies or pastimes?

What has been your most enjoyable or interesting learning experience?

What do you like to read about?

When you open a newspaper, what sorts of stories do you tend to read first?

Personal Abilities

What comes easily or naturally to you?

What would you say is your greatest gift or talent?

What do you excel at when you put forth your best effort?

What are your most well-developed skills?

What has been your greatest accomplishment so far in life?

What about yourself are you most proud?

What would your friends and family say is your best quality?

At what have you had the most success?

In what types of courses do you tend to earn the highest grades?

If you have received any awards or forms of recognition, what have they been for?

Personal Values

What do you really care about?

What would be one thing you really stand for or believe in?

What would you say are the highest priorities in life?

What makes you feel good about yourself when you're doing it?

If there was one thing about the world that you could change, what would it be?

What does living a "good life" mean to you?

How would you define success?

Would you rather be considered smart, wealthy, creative, or caring?

What would you say is your strongest commitment or conviction?

Undergraduate Majors

After you have become aware of your personal interests, abilities, and values, you need to become aware of your options. Here are the majors at CSUB for which you can earn your B.A. or B.S.:

Anthropology

Art

Biology

Business Administration

Chemistry

Child, Adolescent, and Family Studies

Communications

Computer Science

Criminal Justice

Economics

English

Environmental Resource Management

Geology

History

Kinesiology / Physical Education

Liberal Studies

Mathematics

Music

Natural Science

Nursing

Philosophy

Physics

Political Science

Psychology

Public Administration

Religious Studies

Sociology

Spanish

Theater Arts / Drama

Special Major/Interdisciplinary Studies

Students

Fellow students are a great resource, but try to speak with several individuals so that you get a balanced perspective. You could attend a meeting for the major's club (i.e., the English Club), or you could go to a class a few minutes before it starts and ask the students then.

- *What first attracted you to this major?*
- *What do you think are the advantages and disadvantages of majoring in this field?*
- *Knowing what you know now, would you choose this major again?*
- *What course or courses would you recommend if I wanted to get a good sense of the major?*

Faculty

Faculty are another great resource for students, and most faculty will be willing to answer your questions, for every faculty member is interested in increasing the number of majors in the program.

- *What academic skills or qualities does a student need to have in order to succeed in this major?*
- *What are the greatest challenges faced by students majoring in this field?*
- *What do students seem to like the most and the least about majoring in this field?*
- *What can students do with this major after graduation?*
- *What types of graduate programs or professional schools would a student in this major be well prepared to enter?*

Career Counselors: www.csub.edu/cece/students/

An additional resource here on the CSUB campus is our Center for Community Engagement and Career Education (CECE), which offers a variety of inventories and surveys that will help you identify your individual skills and interests, and a counselor will help you connect those skills to a major and career. Visit the CECE site and set up an appointment to meet with an individual advisor.

Considering Your Career

While your major will not define your career, your major will set you down a path that will lead to certain careers more often than others. For example, an English major is much less likely to lead to a career in Astronomy than is a major in Physics.

Consequently, it is a good idea to see what fields and careers a major has led to in the past. Many of CSUB's department homepages give examples of the careers their past graduates have pursued.

The Center for Community Engagement and Career Education (CECE) is another great resource. CECE offers a program called Sigi3 to help you research careers. Additionally, CSUB has worked with University of Tennessee, Knoxville to put together an excellent resource for careers linked to each major. To access these resources, visit www.csub.edu/cece/students

Common Misconceptions about the Major

1. *Picking a major and a career are the same thing.*

Although there is a correlation between majors and careers, there is no one-to-one relationship. Twenty different students with the same major could have twenty completely different jobs. Some careers, like Law, have no prerequisite major. A student could major in English or Mathematics and go on to become a lawyer. Furthermore, many corporations actively seek a diversity of perspectives, so they choose a variety of majors when they make hiring decisions.

2. *My major will determine what I do for the rest of my life.*

Within ten years of graduation, most people are working in careers that are not directly related to their college majors. Just like students change majors, people change careers, and while your major might affect your career, it will by no means be what defines your career (unless that is what you want it to do).

3. *Choosing one major means giving up all the others.*

Actually, there are many ways a student can choose multiple subjects to study. One option is to double-major. Another option is to take multiple minors. A third option is to craft a Special Major in Interdisciplinary Studies whereby a student crafts a unique major that specifically connects two or more fields of study.

Testimonial: Recent CSUB Graduate Eman Shurbaji

When I was choosing my major for college, I thought about what majors would pertain to understanding the nature of man. I initially chose to major in biology, yet later decided to minor in it and switch over to a major in the humanities. While in college, I quickly realized that communicating effectively and efficiently are valuable tools no matter the major of interest. So, I later decided to major in communications with a concentration in journalism. Journalists, like scientists, are inquisitive and look for answers; writing is a creative process that can answer (or leave unanswered) fundamental questions about life. I use my skills from the field of communications to help me with my chemistry and biology minors and vice versa.

Finding Your Vocation

Whatever career you may choose for yourself - doctor, lawyer, teacher - let me propose an avocation to be pursued along with it. Become a dedicated fighter for civil rights.

Make it a central part of your life. It will make you a better doctor, a better lawyer, a better teacher. It will enrich your spirit as nothing else possibly can. It will give you that rare sense of nobility that can only spring from love and selflessly helping your fellow man. Make a career of humanity. Commit yourself to the noble struggle for human rights.

You will make a greater person of yourself, a greater nation of your country and a finer world to live in.
                                        —Martin Luther King

There is a vast world of work out there in this country, where at least 111 million people are employed in this country alone - many of whom are bored out of their minds. All day long.

                                        —Richard Nelson Bolles

A man's work is nothing but this slow trek to rediscover, through the detours of art, those two or three great and simple images in whose presence his heart first opened.   —Albert Camus

To find joy in work is to discover the fountain of youth.
                                        —Pearl S. Buck

In the course of our lives, we will cycle through any number of jobs. We will have bills that need to be paid, and in order to pay those bills, we will need to collect a paycheck. However, if we were to win the lottery or otherwise be presented with financial independence, most of us would quit those jobs in a heartbeat.

If a job, then, is a necessary compromise between ourselves and the world, what is a vocation?

A vocation is defined as a "summons or strong inclination to a particular state or course of action." In other words, a vocation is a calling, a course of "work" that we feel drawn to and that gives our life meaning. If we were to win the lottery, most of us would continue in our vocation, as that vocation has become an integral part of our personal identity.

Given that most of us would prefer to spend our times in vocations rather than jobs, how can we make our vocations our jobs?

As with choosing a major, the first step is to follow the old maxim: "know thyself." It's important to know what gives you satisfaction, what makes you feel positive about the world and your place in it. Some of you may find meaning in helping others, others in making new discoveries.

The questions on the first page of this chapter will help you find the major that will be a good fit for you, but the answers to those questions will also start you on the path to finding your vocation.

RunnerLink: The Career Services Management System

Many of you will choose to work part-time jobs while you take courses at CSUB. Others will apply for internships. RunnerLink is a database that links employers and to job seekers at CSUB; RunnerLink provides students full access to available jobs and all events, activities, and happenings related to career development.

To register for RunnerLink, go to www.csub.edu/cece

Building Life Skills: Maintaining Your Financial Health

In 2001, more young people filed for bankruptcy than graduated from college.*1 Furthermore, the average student carries a credit card debt that ranges between $1,518 and $2,226.*2

Why is this a concern?

This debt can force students to take second or third jobs, which affects a student's ability to successfully complete college. Even if the student manages to carry this debt through college successfully, the debt can negatively impact one's ability to establish a career or purchase a home. Finally, financial stress can affect one's mental health, and there have been at least two cases where college students committed suicide in part because of their credit card debt.*2

What can you do to manage your financial health? College is the time to establish positive spending habits, which means making priorities and instituting a plan by which you can remain true to those goals.

CSUB offers a specific class that helps students maintain financial health:

"Managing Your Personal Finances" FIN 100.

*1 Sullivan, Warren, & Westbrook. *The Fragile Middle Class: Americans in Debt.* Yale UP, 2000.

*2 Norvilitis & Santa Maria. "Credit Card Debt on College Campuses: Causes, Consequences, and Solutions." *College Student Journal* Sept. 2002.

Banking and Credit Cards

Checking / debit accounts and credit cards have become a near-essential for today's college student, but there are some strategies you can follow to make sure you remain in control of your finances and not the other way around.

- Get a free checking and savings account. Many banks will offers students deals that waive fees for ATM withdrawals and monthly fees.

- Always be certain how much money you have in your account, and make sure you know what the fees will be if you overdraw your account.

- Try to pay cash for most of your transactions. If you have to use your credit or debit card, ask yourself a question: "Is this purchase really worth it?"

- If you have to have a credit card, make sure you get one with the lowest interest rate possible and no annual fees. The card should have a credit limit only enough to get you by in an emergency.

- Pay credit card bills on time. Companies charge late fees, sometimes as much as $50 per month. And do not go over your credit limit—that offers just one more way for your credit card company to get rich off your poor judgment.

Textbooks

A new textbook can cost you anywhere from $10 to $300, but there are some strategies for easing this essential expense.

- Try to borrow the book from a friend. This won't work if the book is a new edition, but in most cases, the instructor will be using the same book from the previous quarter, so you probably know at least one person who has the book just sitting on the shelf.

- Buy a used textbook. The bookstore sells used texts, but you may find better deals on-line through sites like Amazon.com and Half.com

- Try to check out the book from the library. The library has many of the novels and texts you may be reading in class, but it may not have a copy of your exact textbook, so ask if your professor can place a copy on reserve if the library does not already have a copy on the shelf.

- If you forget the Runner Reader at home, you can check out a copy for two or twenty-four hours from the library's Check Out Desk.

Building Life Skills: Making and Keeping a Budget

A budget helps you to live within your means and keep track of where your money goes. By keeping an up-to-date budget, you will be more likely to have money in your pocket at the end of the month; if you find yourself broke at the end of the month, a budget will help you prioritize your spending so that the next month will find you in better financial straits. Using the grid below, track your spending for a month by keeping all of your receipts. Anticipate what you will spend for each section, and at the end of the month, see how well the actual amount matched the amount budgeted.

College Budget Worksheet		
	Amount Budgeted	Actual Amount
Income		
Grants		
Scholarships		
Employment income (less taxes)		
Student loans		
Other income (Parents…)		
Total		
Expenses		
	Amount Budgeted	Actual Amount
Tuition and fees		
Books and supplies		
Housing		
Rent/Mortgage		
Utilities		
Phone		
Meals/Groceries		
Clothes		
Laundry		
Car		
Gas		
Auto maintenance		
Insurance (Car/Home/Life)		
Credit card payments		
Entertainment		
Other expenses		
Total		
(Difference/shortfall)		

Building Life Skills: Active Listening

Have you ever tried to have a conversation with someone who won't stop looking around the room, who seems to relate everything you say back to his or her own world, or who seems to constantly interrupt you? Isn't it exasperating trying to talk to someone like that?

Listening is one of the most important components of your college career. If you can listen effectively—in class, during office hours, to your friends and class-mates—you will learn faster, decrease study time, and have fewer difficulties that arise from miscommunication.

The goal of active listening is to promote mutual understanding. Rather than hearing bits and pieces of information, when you are actively listening, you are trying to understand what the speaker is trying to say without making any judgments yourself.

Active listening will be essential to you as you listen to lectures in class and as you interact in group discussions and projects.

The Process of Active Listening

- Focus your attention, which means no text-messaging, no doodling, and no completing other work while the person is talking.

- Review mentally what you already know about the subject and context. If you're listening to a lecture, think of how it relates to the last lecture.

- Avoid distractions, such as a noisy neighbor or a busy window.

- Set aside your opinions and preconceived notions; listen without bias to what the person is saying about the subject.

- Use non-verbal communication to show that you are listening; research has shown that 80% of communication is non-verbal, so make eye-contact, smile, laugh, tilt your head, nod or shake your head (when appropriate) to show you're listening.

- Be actively involved; respond to the speaker's questions or open-ended comments.

When the speaker ends the lecture or discussion,

- Restate the key points to be sure you understand.

- Ask questions for further clarification.

- Synthesize the information with other relevant information (from the class or from current events).

Putting Skills to Work: Active Listening

1. Get into groups.

2. Have each group member choose a different quote from the previous page.

3. Silently, take notes as to what you think the quote means and how it applies to the differences between a job and a vocation. Think of examples from your life and from people you know.

4. Share your quote with the group.

5. Listen to the other group members discuss their quotes.

6. Restate what you see to be the speaker's key points: "so what you are saying is…"

7. Ask a question about the group member's example.

8. Synthesize the quote with one or more of the other quotes.

Chapter Six:
Getting Involved

One of the most important lessons we hope you'll learn at CSUB is the importance of connecting to a community.

There are numerous options for you to get involved in clubs and organizations at CSUB. If you decide to use your college years as a time to merely take courses, choose a major, and get a degree that prepares you for an occupation, you will be missing our on what could be a rewarding extra-curricular life.

There are a myriad of reasons to involve yourself in campus life. Becoming involved in campus organizations will introduce you to new people, teach you the value of political affiliations, deepen your spiritual journey, or help you learn invaluable skills that may prove useful in the future as well as bolstering your résumé.

The purpose of this chapter is to convince you that a crucial part of being a successful student is being an active member of a wider community.

Bowling Alone . . .

In 1995 Robert Putnam wrote an article entitled "Bowling Alone." He found that more and more people were bowling in the 1990s while fewer were bowling in leagues. Putnam argued that our society was becoming isolated and disconnected, In essence, we are a society of people who "bowl alone."

On college campuses, fewer students are involved in campus organizations. Does that make the college experience a more isolated and disconnected one?

According to Putnam, it does. In fact, Putnam argues that the foundation of our democracy may be threatened by such over-emphasis on individuality at the expense of association with others.

In this chapter, we will encourage you to avoid "bowling alone" by associating yourself with campus organizations.

CSUB Student Activities

Hopefully, you have discovered that there is much more to college life than going to class and returning home. All universities offer their students the opportunity for growth--not only intellectually through the curriculum, but socially as well. It's important to make new friends, to enjoy yourself, to learn outside the classroom, and to be part of making things happen on campus. This, in part, is why individuals join the many clubs and organizations we have at CSUB.

Since clubs and organizations help meet the social, educational, recreational, and cultural needs of students on campus, we recognize the important part they play in educational opportunities of students. CSUB currently has 90 registered clubs and organizations focusing on diverse interests or common goals. All offer students an opportunity to become involved on campus with their peers, instructors, and the university itself.

CSUB also has a great intramural program that allows students to become involved in an athletic activity that allows for personal growth, meeting new people and having fun! Please take a moment to browse through our website, contact us at (661) 654-3091, or stop by our office located within the Student Union building.

Clubs and Organizations

One great way to learn more about your desired field of study, to connect with professors and students in the field, and to broaden your understanding and involvement in what may someday be your career is to join (or even create) an academic club.

Another option within your chosen department, once you make that decision, may be to join the honor's society or association affiliated with your major. This is another opportunity to connect with others in your field and to expand your intellectual horizons.

CSUB Blue Crew

The CSUB Blue Crew has been changing the public presence of this school at sporting events and other gatherings by reinvigorating the school spirit and revolutionizing the community. The stands of many CSUB sporting events are seas of blue. Why not join the group? Members of the Blue Crew have one thing in common: pride in their school. CSUB's Student-Athletes Advisory Committee helped to formulate the idea for this version of the Blue Crew. Become a part of a winning team and join the Blue Crew this year!

ACADEMIC/HONORS

1. Alpha Chi National Honor Society
2. Alpha Phi Sigma, Criminal Justice Honor Society
3. Anthropology Club
4. Art Club
5. Association of Student Theatrical Artist (ASTA)
6. Biology Club
7. California Nursing Student Association (CNSA)
8. Chi Alpha Epsilon, Beta Upsilon Chapter
9. Club Literario "Hermes"
10. Club "Soc", Sociology
11. Educational Counseling Association (ECA)
12. English Club, Antelope Valley
13. English Club, CSUB
14. Financial Management Association (FMA)
15. French Club
16. Geology Club
17. History Club
18. Lambda Alpha Rho
19. Management Information System (MIS)
20. Math Club
21. PEAK Majors Club
22. Philosophy and Religious Studies Club
23. Physics Honor Society
24. Pre-Nursing Club
25. Psi Chi National Honor Society in Psychology
26. Psychology Club, Antelope Valley
27. Psychology Club, CSUB
28. Public Relations Student Society of Ame. (PRSSA)
29. Social Work Club
30. Sports Management Club
31. Students Affiliates American Chemical Society
32. University Accounting Association

FRATERNITIES SORORITIES

Greek Council

Delta Zeta Tau **ΔZT**	Gamma Phi Beta **ΓΦB**
Kappa Alpha Order **KA**	Kappa Delta Nu **KΔN**
Kappa Alpha Psi **KAΨ**	Nu Phi Chi **NΦX**
Kappa Sigma Colony **KΣ**	Phi Sigma Sigma **ΦΣ**
Theta Chi **ΘX**	Theta Sigma Chi **ΘΣX**

MULTICULTURAL

1. African American Student Union (AASU)
2. Black Men on Campus (BMOC)
3. Black Women on Campus (BWOC)
4. Filipino-American Association "Kaibigan"
5. International Students Club
6. Japan and Beyond
7. Mariachi Cuicatli
8. M.E.Ch.A
9. Mexica Tiahui Ballet Folklorico

POLITICAL

College Democrats   College Republicans

RELIGIOUS

1. American Muslim Student Association
2. Campus Crusade for Christ
3. Catholic Newman Club
4. Intervarsity Christian Fellowship

SOCIAL SUPPORT

1. Academic Advancement Center Peers (AAC)
2. Child Development
3. Gay/Lesbian/Straight Student Networking (GLSSN)
4. Hispanic Scholarship Fund Chapter
5. Mini-Corps
6. Nursing Class of 2006, 2007, 2008
7. Panhellenic Council *(ΓΦB and ΦΣΣ)*
8. Residential Assistant Club (RA)
9. Residence Hall Association (RHA)
10. Student Activities Club (SAC)
11. Student Ambassadors for Farmworkers
12. Student Council for Exceptional Children
13. The Student Union Club, Antelope Valley
14. Trio Parapros Club
15. Women's Network

SPECIAL INTEREST/OTHER

Global Affairs	Hip Hop	Hogward Honour Society
Hype Squad	Jazz Club	Mad Scientist Society

Media and Technology Club

National Org. for the Reform of Marijuana (NORML)

Student Health Outreach Team (SHOT)

SPORTS AND RECREATION

Fencing Club	Judo Club
Students Athletic Advisory Council (SAAC)	
Triathlon Club	Ultimate Frisbee Club

http://www.csub.edu/StudentActivities/club.shtml

Earth Day

Rebecca Hewett's English 110 Class
Rafer Johnson Day

Psychology Club
Habitat for Humanity
Arvin, CA

Biology Club, Club Day

Celebrate CSUB Day

CSUB Judo Club

College Assistance Migrant Program
NAMIC Awards Show

The Arts at CSUB

There are many reasons to attend the performances at CSUB. The most important is to encourage the development of well rounded students. The sign of any successful society is the arts. Unfortunately, attending the theatre or musical events generally costs a lot of money. At CSUB, students can see classic and contemporary works performed at a fraction of the price. Nowhere but at a university can a student see works by Shakespeare, Moliere, and Lorca, or musical presentations of Puccini and Mozart for under ten dollars. Why not get the full experience of attending a university? It is important to not only nourish the brain with information, but to nourish the spirit with art. Who knows what you may discover . . .

—*Theater Professor Maria-Tania Becerra*

Scene from production of
Antigone in New York

Poster for Senior Exhibition
Spring 2008

CSUB Journals and Magazines

CSUB has a variety of journals and magazines with which students can be involved either as editors or contributors. While *Hermes* and *Orpheus* provide an outlet for personal expression, *Calliope* and *The Kern Economic Journal* are excellent avenues for exploring one's critical faculties, and *The Runner* allows for both journalistic experience and a means of contributing to the on-going discussion as to what it means to be part of the CSUB community.

The Runner

"Newspaper Production" (Communications 214 / 414) is devoted to the production of *The Runner*, the CSUB campus newspaper. Students involve themselves in the reporting, writing, editing and design of the newspaper as appropriate to their interests and assignments. Students operate Macintosh computers in all phases of the production effort. Software programs used include Microsoft Word, QuarkXpress 6.5, Photoshop 7.0 and Photoshop CS2. In addition to the print edition of *The Runner,* students also have an opportunity to become involved in the production of the on-line edition of the newspaper, including the use of video and other multi-media elements. In the production of the on-line edition of *The Runner*, known as "RunnerO," students have the opportunity to utilize Dreamweaver, Flash and Final Cut Express. (www.csub.edu/RUNNER)

The Kern Economic Journal

The Kern Economic Journal, published through the School of Business and Public Administration, is a quarterly publication of California State University, Bakersfield. Its purpose is to track local trends and analyze regional, national, and global issues that affect the economic well-being of Kern County. The journal provides useful information and data that can help the community make informed economic decisions.

(www.csub.edu/kej)

Hermes

Students publish a bilingual literary magazine called *Hermes* by enrolling in General Studies 290. To enroll in this course, students must belong to Club Literario "Hermes" under the advisorship of Dr. Helia M. Corral, Department of Modern Languages and Literatures. The club raises funds; sponsors workshops, lectures, and conferences on reading, writing, editing, publishing, and literature; organizes cultural fieldtrips; and participates in CSUB's student life.

Orpheus

Orpheus is an annual literary journal that publishes short stories, paintings, poems, and other creative work. Copies are available in the Runner Bookstore and the English Department Office in Faculty Towers.

For more information, go to

http://www.csub.edu/english/orpheus.htx

Calliope

Calliope is an annual journal that publishes essays and articles about literary history and criticism. Copies are available in the English Department.

For more information, go to

http://www.csub.edu/English/calliope.htx

Internships, Volunteer Opportunities, and Service Learning

Academic and paid internships give students the opportunity to apply knowledge to real world situations within businesses, agencies, and organizations located throughout the Bakersfield community.

The Center for Community Engagement and Career Education (CECE) is the primary resource for students to review internship and volunteer postings through the university career services management system, RunnerLink, available at www.csub.edu/cece.

Great networking opportunities are created through volunteering and interning! It's not unusual for students to receive job offers as a result of an internship or volunteer experience. Volunteering and serving as an intern enhances your resume and provides you with a valuable opportunity to grow professionally. Service learning is another way for students to gain experience. Service learning is initiated by professors who incorporate an applied experience as a part of the course design. Service learning will also add value to your professional development. To review internship and volunteer opportunities, please visit www.csub.edu/cece and register to use the RunnerLink system. CECE is located in 54 CAF, just next to the Runner Café. CECE can also be reached at 654-3033.

Remember - Experience Matters! You will be more interesting to potential employers and graduate schools if you have invested in applied experiences during your undergraduate program.

Being Involved: A 2010-2011 Testimonial

My name is Amy Aupperle, and for my CSUB volunteer experience, I participated in the Campus Beautification day; this is where we all formed groups to clean up the campus and make a better living environment for residences and off campus students. There were three groups: one group went to prune the rose brushes around campus, the second group went to go plant trees and shrubs around the dorms, and the third group did trash pick-up wherever they felt needed a good cleaning. I chose to be in the second group because I like to plant trees and plants and I live in the dorms, so I want it to look as beautiful as possible not only for myself but for my fellow residents. This experience was a lot of fun due to the amount of people that participate in the event, and the other nice thing about this event is you can work as long as you like. Due to the amount of people that participated, I got to make some new friends and a lot of people that had been a part of this event in the past were sharing stories of how it was like the year before.

I also volunteered for the Providence blood drive because I aspire to be is a nurse and specialize in neonatal nursing (working with newborn babies). One of my friends donates his blood and time into this event many times out of the year. This is how I got involved in this particular blood drive; it was located at my friend's church. I showed up at the blood drive at 8:30 am. It was freezing, so we had to set the chairs out in the sun because that is where it is the warmest; this was one way where we had to accommodate our guests to make sure they were getting the most out of there experience with our blood drive. Before they donate blood, they must fill out a form that makes sure that they are healthy and don't have contaminated blood, due to traveling or piercings or even just having the common cold. When they are called into the truck, the nurses review the form and the patient's iron level has to be checked; if the iron level is too low, then the guest cannot donate, due to the high risk of fainting and other severe injuries. We provide the patients with snacks and juice when they got out of the donation truck; this was to stabilize them after losing a big amount of blood. They have to wait 15 minutes after donating to make sure they aren't dizzy or feeling nauseous. Once they have waited the proper amount of time they are free to leave.

Being a volunteer has given me unique experiences and the satisfaction of doing something good for my community. Volunteering has always been fun, and the nice thing about volunteering is that even if school and work is in the way, it isn't mandatory to attend volunteer work. But being a volunteer is also about being driven for your community and its well-being. I would recommend volunteering wherever people need help because I like to put myself in other people's shoes and wonder if anyone would give me help if I needed it. That's what inspires me to do the right thing, for that is the mind of a volunteer: going above and beyond your own needs.

Make a Difference Day

Saturday, October 22, 2011
Get involved!
Serve your community!
Spend time with your CSUB 101 classmates!

Where can I/we do community service?

- Bakersfield Homeless Center
- Boys and Girls Clubs of Kern County
- Your local park
- Kern County Libraries
- Multiple Sclerosis (MS) Society of Kern County
- Your church
- Get more ideas in your CSUB 101 class!

What kinds of service can I/we do?

*Read to children   *Clean the campus   *Paint
*Landscape *Participate in the MS Walk   *Visit elders
*Assist agencies with special projects
* Get more ideas in your CSUB 101 class!

Make a Difference Day is sponsored by *USAWeekend Magazine*. Students will report their service to their CSUB 101 instructors. We will then submit all of our activities to the sponsoring organization, to enter their competition. If we win, we will have the opportunity to designate a charity that will receive $10,000!

Let's get out and Serve!

Building Life Skills: Effective Communication

College is a time of papers and essays, so it is essential that you acquire and practice effective skills for written communication.

Equally important is your acquisition and practice of oral communication skills. Whether you are discussing a topic with a classmate, responding to a question from the instructor, collaborating on a group assignment, or giving a speech or presentation, the ability to communicate clearly, concisely, and persuasively is an essential component of college education.

In order to emphasize this importance, many professors will include oral communication as part of your overall grade. They may label this work as "Class Participation" or require a speech as a component of the final paper. In fact, when professors have a grade for "Attendance," they are really grading on this give-and-take contribution to the class that can only take place if you are in the classroom and actively contributing to the on-going debate and discussion.

Interpersonal Skills

Your college professors will frequently require you to work on group projects. These might be informal group discussions, or they might be formal 20 page research papers you write in collaboration with other students.

Your professors do not assign group projects in order to torture you. Rather, collaboration is essential to many projects in both the academic and business world. In fact, if you examine scholarly articles, you'll find many that feature two, three, four, and sometimes more authors. This collaborative effort leads to a more diverse final product, as each author or contributor brings his or her own personal strength and insight to the paper or project.

Contributing to Class Discussions

Your professors expect you to ask questions in class. Some professors prefer you ask these questions in the middle of the lecture, and some professors prefer you wait until the lecture ends before you ask the questions. This is something you can ask the professor on the first day of class: "If I have a question during your lecture, should I ask it right away, or should I wait until the lecture is over?"

When you ask a question, be sure your question is on-topic; don't ask a question that pertains to a different subject. Don't ask questions during class that would be better posed during office hours or after class. Pay attention to others' questions; they may have asked the very same question that you have been pondering.

Group Etiquette

- Stay on task; avoid having a group discussion devolve into a social exchange.

- Allow each member to contribute to the discussion and take turns speaking; don't interrupt.

- If a group member is silent, ask him or her questions; don't allow a student to mentally check-out of your group.

- Question facts and debate details; don't engage in personal attacks or criticisms.

- Be sure each member contributes equally; don't become the person in charge of everything, and don't let someone else assume that mantle.

- Set clear roles and goals; if one person is the reporter, then another person should be the presenter.

- Take personal responsibility; don't blame others for a group shortcoming.

- Be proactive; if a group member isn't being responsible, hold him or her accountable before the project is due.

Public Speaking Etiquette

- Project your voice. You are speaking to the entire room, so make sure the entire room can hear you.

- Maintain eye contact with the audience, and be sure to make a visual connection with a person in each part of the room.

- Respond to audience-response; if they look confused, spend more time clarifying and explaining.

- Pay attention to your non-verbal communication. Use hand gestures to emphasize important points, and don't be afraid to move from behind the podium to emphasize information.

- Use notes for assistance and reminders. Reading from your notes is one of the deadliest sins of public speaking, but it is just as damaging to lose your train of thought. Clear, concise, bulleted notes will ensure that you keep focus while avoiding the trap of purely reading.

- Avoid using filler words that are common in conversation but are inappropriate for public speaking: "uh…," "um…," "like, you know…"

- Maintain a professional demeanor: don't chew gum, don't play with your hair, and don't hitch up your belt.

Managing Stress with Public Speaking

Millions of Americans suffer from *Glossophobia*. What is this fearsome disease? It is the fear of public speaking. Some people call it "stage fright," and we all experience it to some degree; in its mildest form, it is the butterflies in the pits of our stomachs when we have to go to the board to complete the latest algebraic equation.

The first thing to remember is that you're not alone; the person before you was nervous, and the person after you is nervous.

The second thing to remember is that these nervous people are probably thinking about themselves: either "Wow, I'm glad that's over" or "I hope I don't mess up, I hope I don't mess up." In other words, your harshest judge is going to be yourself.

Finally, the silver lining is that, as with most things (not including root canals), it gets easier. The fourth speech will be easier than the third, and by the time you graduate from college, your *Glossophobia* will likely be relegated to a minor and infrequent irritation.

Speech Anxiety

- Find your voice in the class before you have to give a speech. This will raise your comfort level with the material, the instructor, and the class so that you will be more prepared for occasions where you have to speak.

- Practice giving a speech in the same room in which you'll be presenting; this will allow you to become more familiar and comfortable.

- Practice using your "Speaker's Voice," which will make you more familiar and comfortable with the sound of your own voice.

- Practice in front of a mirror. You will notice that even though you may feel nervous, you don't look nervous at all.

- Use diversions. Handouts and Powerpoints keep the audience's attention off you, which should ease your stress.

- Maintain regular breathing. While shallow breaths make your body more anxious, deep breaths will help to keep you calm.

- Ignore the signs of stress. Yes, your hands may be shaking. Yes, you may be sweating. So what? Everyone's hands shake. Everyone sweats.

- Keep it in perspective. It's just a speech.

Book Clubs

Another way of fostering connections is to create a book club. These groups are an excellent way to further your knowledge in specific areas or to discuss issues with people who have similar interests.

Many people have found that they learned more from their book clubs than they did from the discussions in class, for these book clubs allow for greater focus on specific passages without the threat of exams or assignments staring them in the face.

Many departments and departmental clubs have their own book clubs. For example, the Philosophy Department has a reading group studying the philosopher Hegel, and the Philosophy and Religious Studies Club has a discussion group focusing on Lyotard's *The Postmodern Condition*.

On a more lighthearted note, there is a CSUB Passions course devoted to the Harry Potter series.

Starting a book club is easy. Your club can focus on a specific area of interest for a class, for a major, or merely for entertainment. Often, your professors will be open to joining these clubs on certain meetings to provide another voice for context and explanation. Once you have your focus, decide on a schedule. Most groups meet once a week or twice a month, as any longer will be too long between discussions and any shorter will not allow people the time to do the critical reading necessary for the discussion. For the meetings themselves, each member should come with specific questions they

CSUB Scavenger Hunt

Grab a partner or two and a digital camera, and explore CSUB.

1. Find your favorite art exhibit on campus. Take a picture of you posing in front of it.

2. Go to Dorothy Donohue Hall, and take your picture in front of your favorite club announcement (based on the quality of their display).

3. Go to one of the CSUB athletics practice facilities. Take a picture of yourselves in action.

4. Take a picture of yourselves playing air guitar (or another instrument of your choice) in front of the Doré Theater.

5. Take a picture of yourselves acting out a scene from your favorite play in front of the Doré Theater.

6. Review the calendar of events (under Campus Events on the drop-down box on the CSUB homepage). Choose one event to attend.

Furthering Campus Excellence

1. Get into groups and choose a section of camps.

2. Explore that area of campus.

3. Take note of the types of interactions that are (and are not) occurring.

4. What changes would you make to this section of campus to improve the quality of student life?

5. How should CSUB go about implementing these changes?

6. What changes should CSUB implement to improve the quality of student life overall?

7. Present your recommendations to the class.

Chapter Seven: Celebrating Difference

Benefits of Diversity

Recent studies* have found a consistent correlation between diversity in higher education and both effective learning and democracy. In other words, diversity in college helps the individual student learn more effectively and helps the state of the country overall.

How does this work?

First of all, for many students, college is the first time they're exposed to life different from their home communities, and young people's social identities are still in flux, which means that they're in a crucial stage of social development wherein assumptions can be challenged or made more entrenched. In other words, if a student overcomes bias now, then that person will probably be open-minded for the rest of his or her life. On the other hand, if a student's biases are not challenged and overcome, then that person may harbor those biases for the rest of his or her life.

Secondly, by its very nature, college should be diverse and complex enough to allow for intellectual experimentation. It is no coincidence that many scientific breakthroughs

happen in colleges and universities, for through intellectual experimentation, researchers are able to make connections that otherwise would be overlooked.

Similarly, complex thinking occurs when a person is challenged and has no rote or learned intellectual response on which to fall back. In other words, complex thinking happens when a person must objectively evaluate and consider all points of view, something that is less likely to happen if a person is not open to other perspectives.

Finally, diversity competence is one of the hallmarks of a successful democracy. A person who is knowledgeable about other social groups will be less likely to be swayed by prejudice; this person will be more likely to make objective civil decisions, whether it is voting or serving on a jury.

On a purely economic level, having a greater degree of diversity competence enables you to more successful interact with diverse groups of people.

*Expert Report of Patricia Gurin. Gratz, et al. v Bollinger, et al. No. 97-75321. United States District Court. Eastern District of Michigan. 1997.

The Consequences of Lack of Diversity

What constitutes diversity? At one level, any variation could constitute diversity, and in that sense, there is never homogeneity (with an exception, perhaps, in cloning).

One difficulty in dividing and classifying people into groups is that this labeling presents a question: "Who gets to decide the categories?"

Historically speaking, race and religion have been the two categories most fraught with conflict and prejudice: wars

(and holocausts) have been waged because one race or religion was deemed "lesser" by a dominant group.

Hate crimes continue to this day, as do more subtle forms of discrimination in employment and housing. Ultimately, this can lead to frustration, backlash, and social disorder.

Our brains have evolved to make us relate to those who look and behave like we do, so it is not an easy task to overcome our biases, but it is essential that we make the attempt.

California State University, Bakersfield Demographics, Fall 2010

Statistics taken from CSU Bakersfield Fast Facts

GENDER DIVERSITY

Men	2,469	38%
Women	4,081	62%

AGE DIVERSITY

Under age 24	4,520	69%
Age 24 and older	2,030	31%

ETHNIC DIVERSITY

Undergraduates

American Indian	91	1%
Asian, Pacific Islander, Filipino	538	7%
African American	595	8%
Latino or Hispanic	3,238	41%
White	2,424	31%
Multiple Races	115	1%

FIRST-TIME FRESHMEN PROFILE

Institution of Origin

Kern County Public Schools	790	78%
Other California Public Schools	213	20%
Other States	10	1%
Other Countries	20	1%

Diversity at CSUB

One clear measure of CSUB's diversity is to look at the list of clubs.

There are clubs that showcase our ethnic diversity: Filipino-American Association "Kaibigan," Black Men and Women on Campus (BMOC & BWOC), M.E.Ch.A, and Japan and Beyond.

Some clubs focus on politics, such as College Democrats and Republicans, while other clubs illustrate our religious diversity: American Muslim Student Association, Campus Crusade for Christ, and Catholic Newman Club.

Gay/Lesbian/Straight Student Networking (GLSSN) illustrates our sexual diversity.

A panoply of clubs showcase the diversity of interests, careers, and helping professions: Women's Network, Child Development, Student Ambassadors for Farmworkers, Global Affairs, Hip Hop, and Philosophy and Religious Studies Club.

Another measure of CSUB's diversity is illustrated through its published demographics.

The greatest measure of CSUB's diversity probably rests in its age breakdown; roughly half of CSUB's student population is under 24. What this means is that CSUB has a solid population of students returning to college after spending some time in the workplace.

According to 2000 U.S. Census data, the city of Bakersfield has a population that breaks down as follows:

Latino	32.5%
White	51.1%
Black	9.2%
Asian	4.3%
Native American	1.4%
Other	1.5%

This population generally reflects the population at CSUB, which isn't surprising given that over 80% of the first-time freshmen CSUB population comes from Kern County.

In terms of faculty diversity, according to the Fall 2009 Faculty and Staff Profile, the demographics of faculty is as follows:

Latino	51
White	321
Black	21
Asian	44
Native American	2
Other	2
Women	235
Men	206

CSUB actively works to foster diversity, as one of President Mitchell's goals is to have "faculty and academic excellence and diversity" such that "the content of courses, curricula, and degree programs reflect a diversity of intellectual thought."*

* "Our Vision." California State University. Office of the President.

Race, Ethnicity, and Culture

One of the difficulties in describing race, ethnicity, and culture is that the definitions are fluid and somewhat subjective.

Today, race is generally used to describe the shared genetic code among a group of peoples. In other words, based on our DNA, we belong to a code shared among a group of people who originated in a certain part of the world. Thus, race generally refers to the part of the world from which your ancestors originated: African, Asian, European, Native American. However, this coding is problematic in that most people are a mix of different genetic codes, and historically speaking, people have never been completely static; in this way, DNA can be both extremely precise and narrow down a person's ancestry to a specific mountain range, but it can also illustrate a person's background as a multitude of locations.

Ethnicity today refers to shared national origins or cultural patterns. Thus, we have African Americans, Italian Americans, and Hispanic Americans.

Culture is even more specific and refers to shared cultural products, attitudes, and characteristics. For example, in America people in the south have a culture distinct from those of the northwest, which is illustrated in music, dress, and regional holidays.

The problem with these definitions is that they are subjective. To someone who isn't from America, a Mexican-American and a Cuban-American might appear identical, but to anyone from either of those two ethnicities, the differences would be profound.

Prejudice, Bias, and Stereotypes

Stereotypes occur because our minds like and need patterns in order to store information, but stereotypes are damaging in that they reduce individuals to a crude definition, and anyone who has experienced stereotyping can tell you that it is an often dehumanizing experience. Prejudice and stereotypes can occur with all difference: gender, race, religion, and ethnicity.

The problem, of course, is that stereotypes are often inaccurate: blondes can be intelligent, and white men can jump. Prejudice often starts at an unconscious level, so it's important that we be honest about our own generalizations and misconceptions about others. Be sure to evaluate individuals as individuals, and beware of making judgments of a whole group of people based on your experiences with one or two individuals.

Developing Cultural Competence

- Talk to individuals from other cultures. If you have a question about their culture, ask.

- Learn about other cultures through their art and literature.

- Offer to share your culture with others. Recommend books and music, and offer information about holidays and important figures.

- CSUB has a number of lecture series wherein distinguished individuals from around the world come and share their thoughts. Attend these lectures and think about how their insights pertain to your life.

- Travel. There is no better way to learn about others than to experience those cultures firsthand. An added benefit to making friends from other countries is that you'll have a friendly tour guide when you visit.

- Be open to life's experiences. You never know when you'll have the opportunity to meet new people or experience diversity, so remain open-minded.

Maximizing the Benefits of Diversity in the Classroom

- Present your viewpoints in a respectful manner, and don't get angry if someone disagrees with you.

- Be tolerant of others' perspectives. If someone voices a perspective that you think is weak, focus on the specific aspects of that argument that are weak rather than declaring the entire perspective wrong.

- Begin with appeals to common ground. In discussions, start with perspectives on which you all agree. This will create an atmosphere that will be more conducive to open and healthy disagreement.

- Don't assume you can understand what it's like to be a member of another group. A man can never know exactly what it's like for a woman, and an African American can never know exactly what it's like for a Native American. It is arrogant (and misguided) to assume you know what others have gone through unless you have experienced those things yourself.

- Don't treat individuals as spokespersons for the group. Don't ask a man what it's like for all men, and don't ask a Muslim to explain the Muslim experience. All experiences are individual and unique even if they fit within and exemplify general patterns.

- Seek out students who are different from you. The most effective and insightful projects and papers often result from diverse groups. These differences can be in age, gender, ethnicity, religion, or major.

Questions to Consider

1. What are the benefits of having a substantial population of students returning to college after spending time in the workplace?

2. Roughly 14% of CSUB students declined to state their ethnicity. What do you think explains this statistic?

3. What are the benefits and drawbacks from having over 80% of first-time freshmen coming from Kern County?

4. How can CSUB increase its diversity?

5. How can CSUB emphasize the diversity it already has?

Putting Skills to Work: Group Diversity

1. Make a list of all the different identities to which you belong: ethnicity, gender, religion, age, major, and so on.

2. Get into groups of five wherein each group member represents an identity different from the other four individuals.

3. If these were the demographics of a company or organization, how would your individual differences make the group stronger? Be specific and give examples.

Study Abroad

Have you ever dreamed of wandering the streets of Rome, Tokyo, Paris, or Incheon? As a CSUB student you have that opportunity through the Study Abroad program. This year, 17 CSUB students will be studying in places as diverse as Korea, Germany, Japan, France, and Spain.

Why Study Abroad?

1) It is the optimal and easiest way to learn another language. Being immersed in the country and culture of the language you are trying to learn is the best approach!

2) Study abroad increases your chances for employment and a promising career. Observe the statistics. Only 1% of American students go abroad. There is a big chance that studying aboard will make your resume outstanding and noticed by your future employer.

3) Study abroad expands your worldview, allows you to make friends around the world, and gives you an opportunity to break the academic routine!

Studying Abroad: A 2010-2011 Testimonial

Hi, my name is Angelina Manriquez, and I spent the 2010/2011 school year in Madrid, Spain, which was one of the most amazing and unforgettable experiences in my life! I have not only built life long friendships with the people I've met here but I have also matured in a lot of different ways. I realize that I am a different person, for the better. I've become more responsible, stronger willed, and more open. I've even learned a few words in different languages such as Italian, Portuguese, Romanian, and Arabic. It's been an open door to learn about many cultures and to see many things that I have never even thought about. Tolerance and patience are also two of the most fundamental things that I've learned as I went through this year in Spain. It seemed impossible for me to get the opportunity to study abroad in another country because I am the first generation to go to college, but now it seems impossible for this to end so soon!

This year flew by faster than what I had imagined. I honestly wish every person in this world would get the opportunity to get out of their comfort zone and live in another country for a year. Not everyone gets this privilege, but it's an experience that no one will regret. Sure, there are times when you miss one thing or another, but that's the fabulous function of Skype, Facebook, and all the technology out there that helps you keep in touch with your friends and family. Besides that, there are some amazing people who work with the program and they will help you with anything they can. Because of all the trips that are planned and included in the program, I became attached to everyone in the group, and we became like a big family. At the beginning of the year, I joined a soccer team, and although I've never played before, it was a fun experience because it was through this that I met many Spanish girls who brought me into the Spanish culture. I lived with a roommate and a couple: the man is a Spaniard and the woman is from Peru. They always made us feel at home and offered to answer all the questions we had. They taught us how to cook real Spanish food, how to use words we didn't understand, and how and why things worked the way they did. Honestly, I have never met such a great diversity of people.

This year has helped me be independent and at the same time it helped me define who I am and stand for what I believe. I'm learning to be independent from my family and to separate my job from personal problems. I also learned to manage stress on my own, and it is all part of preparing me for that "real world." I am not as shy as I was before coming here and I have experienced living outside of home away from my family and everything that had surrounded me all my life. I would strongly recommend studying abroad! I believe it is a once in a life time experience and even if you do travel to Spain or any other country some day, coming as a tourist for a few days or weeks cannot compare to living as a resident student for a year and meeting lifelong friends and cherishing memories together. You find yourself discovering things about yourself and building plans for your future along with appreciating even more every moment. It has certainly been one of the best decisions I've made in my life!

CSU-IP (CSU International Programs)

International Programs is the system-wide study abroad program of the California State University. IP is affiliated with over 50 universities and other institutions of higher education in 19 countries. If you dream of travelling to exotic countries, maybe you should consider Australia, Spain, France, Germany, Italy, South Korea, Japan, Chile, Mexico, or Sweden as your destination?

All classes taken abroad will receive credit and it will appear on CSUB transcripts.

Currently in its forty-third year of continuous operation, the academic excellence of IP has been recognized by respected organizations such as the Council of Learning and the Western Association of Schools and Colleges.

Bi-lateral Programs

This program is based on one-to-one exchange of CSUB and affiliated institutions. The student pays CSUB fees and tuition before departure to the host institution. Room and board are arranged through the host institution. Currently CSUB has contracts with: Odense University (Southern Denmark), University the Orleans (France), University of Incheon (South Korea) and Bucheon University (South Korea).

ISEP-Direct Program

If you are not sure of making a commitment for the whole academic year (as IP requires), perhaps you want to go to one of twenty-nine countries available in this newly available opportunity? Have you ever thought about study in Botswana, Argentina, Chile, Belgium, Costa Rica, India, The Netherlands or Brazil for one semester? Since April 2010 the aim of the program is to enable students to broaden their knowledge by enrolling in major related classes while studying abroad. If you want to learn more, please visit:

www.isep.org/direct

Can I afford it? Absolutely! Your financial aid "travels" with you.

The sites below should help you with basic resources:

www.finaid.org   www.edupass.org   www.exchanges.state.gov   www.ssa.gov

How to apply?

Contact information:

If you have additional questions, want to apply or are thinking about going abroad, please contact the International Students and Programs Office at:

dkarnowski@csub.edu

csubis@csub.edu

or call: (661)-654-6113

Chapter Eight:
Study Skills and
Preparing for Finals

How will you prepare for your final exams?

Do you get extra stress when you hear the phrase "final exam"?

Should you prepare differently for a final exam than you do for other exams?

How much extra help can you expect from your professors on your final exams?

If you have more than two exams scheduled on one day is there anything you can do to decrease your burden?

At CSUB, professors offer a wide variety of final exams.

In some cases, your test will simply be the third or fourth "unit" test of the quarter. Your professor might have a part of the exam that covers the last portion of the quarter and a portion that is cumulative or comprehensive, covering the whole quarter. Your final exam might be online or in-class. You may have a final presentation rather than an exam. Your exam may be multiple choice, short answer, essay, fill in the blank, or, if you are taking voice classes, it may be something you sing.

Whatever the case, there are some basic skills and habits that will serve you well as you go through the final examination procedure here at CSUB three times per year for the next four years.

Preparing Begins the First Day of Class

There is a direct relationship between your engagement in a class and your grade in that class. You will have to take many classes in college that seem to have nothing to do with your current or future life. In every class, however, you should be involved in constantly trying to relate the information to your experience, reading, and other classes.

According to Morton Hunt, author of *The Universe Within: A New Science Explores the Mind*, "The extent to which we remember a new experience has more to do with how it relates to existing memories than with how many times or how recently we have experienced it."

In other words, actively link your classes to other information. If you are studying abnormal psychology and think it relates to your boss, write it in your notes and ask your professor about it. If you are studying physics and think about a recent play in football, write it in your notes and ask your professor about it. If you are studying Spanish and are reminded of a movie you saw, write it in your notes and ask your professor about it.

The more you can actively involve learning with what you already know, the more you will remember the new information.

Types of Questions (and How to Answer Them)

Multiple-Choice Questions

Cross off any obviously incorrect answers. If there is an "all of the above" option, you only need to verify that two of the answers are correct to choose that option. Be careful, though. Often, professors will include test questions that are intended to distract your attention from the answer.

When you read the question, try to answer the question in your mind before you read the alternatives.

Finally, ask your professor if you are penalized for guessing. If not, then mark off the obviously wrong answer so that you increase your odds of making a good guess.

Short Answer and Fill-in-the-Blank Questions

Do not turn these questions into brief essays. Clear and succinct answers are best. If you get stumped on a question, read through the rest of the exam looking for clues that may help you. Also, remember to go back and check these answers later. As you work on the exam you may come across other answers in your memory.

Essay Exams

Many of your exams will consist of nothing but essays. You may be asked to write two different responses, or you may be asked to write one four-page response to a specific question. The following pages have information, courtesy of English Instructor Brooke Hughes, designed to help you navigate these timed-writing essay exams.

True / False Questions

Look for universals. Many times, if the question has an "always" or "never" statement in it, it is false. (That's not "always" true, though.)

Don't over-analyze the questions. Remember, if you have studied and attended class, then you are probably going to recognize the correct answer. Honor your own gut reaction to the question.

Essay Questions

Many courses at CSUB end with an essay exam.

Usually, because of our two-and-a-half hour final exam structure, you will have enough time to complete your essay. Read the question twice. A fantastic essay that does not answer the question will not pass. Next, you should do a brief brainstorm and create a simple outline to give yourself a plan of where to proceed with your essay.

Write a clear introduction that clearly illustrates that you understand the essay question. If the essay calls for it and the professor has emphasized it, make a clear argument. Essays that prove something or persuade are much better written and much more readable than those that simply describe. Be sure to provide a conclusion that reiterates your main point clearly and succinctly.

If possible, double-space your essay. If you have trouble writing legibly (slowing down will help with this), double spacing your essay may help. Double-spacing will also allow for easier reading and will also give you space if you need to add information later. Be sure to include clear, specific detail and concrete examples in your answer. Finally, proofread your essay. Even on a timed essay, you should use your time wisely, leaving a few minutes at the end for re-reading. Correcting simple mistakes can make a big difference.

Read and Understand the Question or Prompt

The most common, and worst, mistake that you can make when writing with a time limit is to misread the question. You may feel that you need to rush and get started, but once you get your assignment, take a deep breath, and slow down. To craft an accurate response, you must know where to begin as well as where you're going. An effective strategy is to underline, circle, or otherwise highlight the key verbs/words in the question. Below are explanations of the words and phrases you'll find in instructions for timed essays:

- **Agree or disagree:** Take a position and stick with it throughout the entire essay. Don't change your mind or try to argue both sides.

- **Challenge:** This term is a synonym for disagree.

- **Compare:** Outline the similarities between the two sides.

- **Contrast:** Outline the differences between the two sides.

- **Compare and contrast:** The expectation is that you do both, not choose one.

- **Debate:** You can argue both sides of the topic. Ultimately, though, develop a specific position with one side coming out stronger.

- **Define:** Outline the topic's main points.

- **Illustrate:** Make a point and use specific examples to support it.

- **Identify parallels:** This phrase is a synonym for compare.

- **Develop your point of view:** This is what you'll be asked to do for many timed writing situations. You may use any of the strategies listed above to support a thesis that takes a position on the topic.

- **Discuss** or **explain:** If you see these terms, you'll want to use a combination of the other processes; you might want to define, challenge, and compare and contrast.

Plan the Organization of the Essay

Again, you may feel the urge to rush ahead. Yet if you do so without devising some sort of design, you are almost certain to lose focus and end up with a jumble of words that leads nowhere. Writers generally have their own personal strategies, but if you haven't found one that works for you, consider the following techniques:

- Outlining: This format is helpful for people who like clear structure.

- Brainstorming: Put the topic or thesis in the center of the page and then write supporting examples that branch out from the main point.

- Listing: Similar to outlining but with a bit less structure, this method lets you get your ideas down easily.

- Weighing pros and cons or similarities and differences: When you're asked to debate or to compare and contrast two ideas, write a heading for each assertion, draw a line between the headings, and list the main points side by side.

Write the Essay

All essays are comprised of three basic components: the introduction, the body, and the conclusion.

Introduction: An introduction has three parts: the hook, an explanation of background and context, and the thesis.

The hook is a creative start draws readers in and makes them want to keep going. However, unless a great opening dawns on you immediately, skip it, and leave space to go back later (if you have time).

The background and context is to introduce key concepts and relationships that are essential for understanding your paper. For example, if you are writing a literary analysis, part of the background and context would include the author's name and the title of the work you are analyzing.

The thesis statement is the most important part of your essay: it is the essay's raison d'être (reason for being). Without a strong thesis statement, your essay becomes a miscellaneous collection of words and ideas. With a strong thesis statement, your essay will more likely possess a convincing argument.

The thesis statement must contain both the topic and an argument about that topic.

⇒ It must relate to everything your essay contains.

⇒ It must be debatable, that is, it should be a claim that shows independent analysis and is not already self-evident.

⇒ It must be clear and concise. A thesis statement does not need to be limited to one sentence necessarily, but it must not ramble or sprawl.

⇒ It should be logically placed in the essay, usually the introduction and conclusion.

Body: For each body paragraph, include a topic sentence that gives a specific example to prove your thesis statement and a body that elaborates upon or explains this example. Support your thesis with one or two well-developed examples. Be sure that each of your body paragraphs has a specific purpose, and be sure to explain and support that purpose with analysis and examples.

Conclusion: Try to come up with a conclusion that does more than restate your thesis and main points. However, unless your directions require one, a formal conclusion isn't always needed. Your time might be better spent editing and proofreading your essay.

Edit and Proofread the Essay

Try to leave at least 10-15 minutes to read through your entire essay. Look out for any structural or content errors. Then, if time permits, check for spelling and grammatical mistakes. Lastly, if you have time, revisit your introduction to see if you can improve your opening.

Remember, you can write a solid, effective essay in a short time—if you use those precious minutes wisely.

Edit for Content	Proofread for Mechanics
Is your thesis clear and concise?	Have you corrected your fragments and run-on sentences?
Do you have clear topic sentences?	Have you checked your subject-verb agreement?
Do you give examples for your ideas?	Have you checked your punctuation?
Do you provide definitions for key terms?	Have you made sure all your verbs are in the correct tense?
Do you provide transitions between ideas?	Have you checked your spelling?

Timed–Writing Outlines

For a two hour class:

Time Remaining	You should …
1 hour, 45 minutes	begin reading the prompt
1 hour, 30 minutes	begin writing the introduction and thesis
1 hour	begin writing body paragraphs
45 minutes	HALFWAY POINT finish body paragraphs
30 minutes	begin writing the conclusion
15 minutes	begin proofreading
5 minutes	print

For a 90-minute class:

Time Remaining	You should …
1 hour, 20 minutes	begin reading the prompt
1 hour, 10 minutes	begin writing the introduction and thesis
50 minutes	begin writing body paragraphs
35 minutes	HALFWAY POINT finish body paragraphs
20 minutes	begin writing the conclusion
10 minutes	begin proofreading
5 minutes	print

Studying for Finals

Preparing for your exams begins in class. Keep up with your reading, practice active listening during lectures, and review your notes before and after each class.

As you get closer to the final exam date, there are additional strategies you can follow to improve your chances of success.

- **Make Note Cards**: This tried and true method is great for a number of reasons. First, it makes you write out the information you need to learn. That forces you to review the material. Second, learning from note cards is a good study technique for testing yourself.

- **Group Study:** Ask your professor to announce in class that you want to create a study group. You will be pleased with the results.

- **Study Out Loud:** This may make you look ridiculous to your family or roommates, but reviewing your notes out loud is a sure fire way to test yourself and to remember what you've been taught.

- **Create Your Own Test**: Try to anticipate what the instructor will ask. Think about the key themes during the course and especially about the ideas that your professor seemed to repeat.

- **Go to the Review Session**: Many professors offer a review session where students can ask questions. Often, the instructor will give clues as to specific questions on the exam during these sessions.

- **Use Office Hours**: After trying to guess the test, take your questions and go into the professor's office hours. Ask the professor to assess your guesses. You won't get the test handed to you, but you could possible receive invaluable test preparation and hints.

Review Previous Exams

Re-read the comments on previous exams and assignments. If your professor did not make comments, take the exam to her or his office to ask for clarification on how you can improve on the final exam.

If you write an essay question on a previous exam and the professor said you needed to include more detail in your answer, then learn the lesson and be sure to include more detail on the final.

Not learning from your mistakes is extremely frustrating for your professors. In fact, it is not uncommon for a student to miss the exact same question on the final that the student got wrong on an earlier exam! If you can show improvement over the ten week quarter, you are sending the signal that the hard work—both yours and your professors—is paying off.

Blue Books

Many of your professors will require that you complete your final exam in a Blue Book, which is a thin booklet you can purchase in the Runner Bookstore. The Associated Students will often hand Blue Books out for free in the Student Union during finals week.

Be sure to ask if your professor requires a Blue Book for the final exam. If you need one, it sends a bad signal to show up to the final exam empty-handed, and the time you spend running to the bookstore to buy a Blue Book will be that much less time you will be spending completing the exam.

Building Life Skills: Mnemonic Devices

Using Acronyms

Mnemonic Devices are simple memory tools that will help you recall data. There are many techniques to help you do this.

One common mnemonic device is to use an acronym, or a word in which each letter stands for a word you need to remember.

Some acronyms are simple and common:

NASA=National Aeronautic and Space Administration

Other acronyms will help with specific classes. For instance, if you are studying psychology and need to remember Elisabeth Kubler-Ross' five stages of death and dying you might create the following acronym:

DABDA= Denial, Anger, Bargaining, Depression, Acceptance

If you need a simple way to remember the five Great Lakes, try HOMES:

HOMES=Huron, Ontario, Michigan, Erie, Superior

Using Acrostics

Another mnemonic device is an ACROSTIC, or a sentence in which the first letter in each word stands for another word you need to remember:

King Philip Came Over For Grape Soda =

Kingdom, Phylum, Class, Order, Family, Genus, Species

A good acrostic for Kubler-Ross might be the following:

Danny and Barry Date Alice = Denial, Anger, Bargaining, Depression, Acceptance

Using Rhyming

If you can turn your class notes into a simple rhyme, you will be much more likely to remember the information.

"Columbus sailed the ocean blue in 1492."

"I Before E except after C"

Those are simple, but you can create your own rhymes or raps to recall intricate information like Newton's law of motion:

" My friend Newton said it best, 'a physical body will remain at rest,' or it'll at least continue on the same path, unless, Newton said, without any wit, an external force acts upon it."

Creative Visualization

During tests, many students will sit and stare at the instructor while he or she is at the front of the room.

When asked later to explain why they were so intensely gazing at the instructor, students respond by saying that they were able to visualize the professor giving the lecture.

How can they do this? First, these students all paid close attention during lecture. This allowed them to build a library of lived experience from which they could later remember the lecture. Second, rather than looking down at the paper during the whole exam, students relaxed and looked up at the front of the room to use their imagination. Staring off into space, or in this case up at the front of the classroom, can be very helpful as a means of accessing information from all parts of your brain.

Neurolinguistics explores the connection between mind and body as regards the acquisition of language and the production of memory. The brain, as you may already know, is broken into left and right spheres. One way to access the material that you have stored in the memory center of your brain is to look up (for most people, up and to the right is the best place to look). This physical action helps your brain retrieve information.

Creative Visualization Exercise

1. Find a partner.

2. Have your partner imagine sitting in a car outside of the Valley Plaza.

3. Have your partner count mentally each stoplight he or she comes to while driving from the Valley Plaza to Cal State.

4. While your partner counts, you simply observe.

5. Now assess what happened: Did your partner look up into space to find any of the stoplights?

More importantly, how can we use this information?

As you are taking exams, you are usually facing down at the exam during the entirety of the test. During the exam, take a simple neurolinguistic break, looking up and slightly to the right to energize all parts of your brain.

Creative Visualization and Remembering Dates

"I'm no good with dates."

If you must remember a number or a date, try to visualize the numbers superimposed over a figure or image that is associated with the information. For example, look at the Mona Lisa to the right. Do you know when Leonardo da Vinci painted this masterpiece? It was 1503.

Stare for 10 seconds at this painting. Now, in your mind, write the number 1503 across her forehead. See the numbers as you write them, raising your finger to write them with an imaginary pen.

Stare at the 1503 on the Mona Lisa's forehead again. Stare at the Mona Lisa's eyes and then look up at the numbers you've written on her forehead.

Look at the Mona Lisa's forehead again. What year was it painted?

This act of mental graffiti is an effective way to remember associations and relationships.

Test Anxiety

Stress is a normal reaction to final exams and can actually improve concentration, focus, and memory. Thus, you should not try to eliminate stress; rather, you should work on keeping stress from becoming anxiety.

Anxiety is a negative mental and emotional state that can interfere with your concentration, memory, and critical thinking. If you experience the following symptoms during tests, then you may be experiencing test anxiety:

- Physical symptoms of a pounding heartbeat, rapid pulse, sweating, or upset stomach.

- Difficulty concentrating or focusing your attention.

- Negative thoughts and emotions (*I can't do this, I'm stupid*).

- Rushing through the test just to get it over with.

- Inability to access information during the test but complete recall once you leave the room.

An important thing to keep in mind is that test anxiety is not equivalent to lack of preparation. Many students blame anxiety for their poor performance when the actual cause of the low score is a lack of effective studying. However, if you practice effective study strategies and still experience anxiety, you can visit the CSUB Counseling Center to get professional advice on how to counter this anxiety:

661-654-3366

Keep to a Familiar Pattern

- Study in the same room in which you'll be taking the exam. Just as there is a "home court advantage" in sports, the same theory applies here. You're more likely to be successful in an environment with which you're familiar.

- Sit in the same seat that you normally take in class. Again, consistency leads to comfort, and there will be many visual clues that you (consciously or unconsciously) used while you were studying in that room that will help you recall information.

- Make sure you eat a healthy meal before the exam. Don't overload on sugars, as that energy will run out halfway through the exam, and you'll experience a crash in energy.

During the Test

- Immediately write down any mnemonic devices or memory-improvement shortcuts you have created. Write down essential names, terms, formulas, and equations that you had to memorize.

- Answer the easy questions first. You don't need to answer the questions in order, and it will be a boost to your self-confidence to immediately start answering the questions you know you'll get right. This will also keep you from getting distracted by and stuck on difficult questions. You may also find clues to those difficult questions in your responses to the easy ones.

- Use creative visualization techniques. Close your eyes and imaging that you're in the room in which you studied or that you're back in time listening to the instructor's lecture. This is called a "guided retrieval" and can often help you access "lost" information.

- Skip to the next question if you get stuck. Often, you have the answer to the previous question stuck in your unconscious, and the answer just needs some time to come to

Testimonial: CSUB and Loyola Marymount Student Laura Flachmann

For me, going into a test that I'm particularly anxious about feels like a boxer has punched me in the stomach, like my legs aren't mine, like all the information in my brain is being overtaken by a tornado, like someone is hammering at a steady pace on my forehead, and like whatever food I just consumed is going to make its way up at a fast speed, and then, the tears start to invade. I get butterflies; my legs are weak and restless; my brain becomes so overrun by emotions and angst that my mind can't focus on the information I need; I get a migraine; I feel nauseous; and all of these symptoms, along with my inability to concentrate and retrieve the necessary information from my knowledge, make me extremely emotional.

I have walked out of tests in the past because my feelings get the best of me and I can't even begin to calm myself down. But these days, I rarely have any problems, which I contribute completely to therapy. My anxiety was taking over my life and causing me to do so poorly in school that I needed to take some action. So I started seeing a therapist to learn how to control my the anxiety. After three months, I can say I'm almost completely calmed down about events that used to upset me. I highly recommend professional help.

If professional help is not an option, I can also suggest some techniques that I learned for relaxing. My psychology professor taught me this first technique. Tighten each part of your body one at a time while inhaling for 10 seconds. Then release and exhale. Repeat each body part twice before moving on to the next part. Include your eyes, lips, face, shoulders, hands, stomach, back, legs, toes, everything. This exercise will teach you how to relax parts of your body you didn't necessarily know were tense in the first place. Once your body parts relax, your mind can relax as well.

One way I taught myself to calm down about tests in particular is, when feeling anxiety come on, I go into a quiet area, find a place to sit, and breathe in and out very slowly. While breathing out, I tell myself that this is just a test; it is important but is not a life or death situation; doing poorly is not the end of the world; everything is going to be fine. And I repeat that in my head over and over while breathing deeply and slowly. After a while, I have convinced myself that everything is fine, and I am actually quite relaxed.

For two years I let my anxiety get the best of me. I never fought it because I never thought I'd win. Then, I finally had enough and knew I had to do something if I ever wanted to make it through school with good grades. So that's when I started trying to find out how my anxiety could be controlled. I've had to be very patient finding something that works every time, but it's definitely worth all the work when I go into a testing situation with just a few butterflies rather than a full-blown panic attack where running seems to be the only route to "safety."

During the Test

- Focus on the test and the individual questions.

Don't worry about what your grade on the exam or the class will be.

Don't worry about whether other students are finishing early; their experience is irrelevant to you.

- Focus on what you know, not on what you don't.

Keep a positive attitude in mind, and continue to access and use all the detail you remember; even if your answer isn't an exact fit, you may get partial credit.

- Keep the test in perspective.

Your exams aren't a measure of how smart you are or aren't, and your grade does not reflect who you are as a person. College exams are meant to be difficult, so don't be discouraged by that difficulty.

Academic Integrity: CSUB Policy

The principles of truth and integrity are recognized as fundamental to a community of teachers and scholars. The University expects that both faculty and students will honor these principles and in so doing will protect the integrity of all academic work and student grades.

Students are expected to do all work assigned to them without unauthorized assistance and without giving unauthorized assistance.

Faculty has the responsibility of exercising care in the planning and supervision of academic work so that honest effort will be encouraged and positively reinforced. There are certain forms of conduct that violate the university's policy of academic integrity.

Academic Dishonesty (Cheating) is a broad category of actions that use fraud and deception to improve a grade or obtain course credit. Academic dishonesty (cheating) is not limited to examination situations alone, but arises whenever students attempt to gain an unearned academic advantage.

Plagiarism is a specific form of academic dishonesty (cheating) which consists of the misuse of published or unpublished works of another by claiming them as one's own. Plagiarism may consist of handing in someone else's work, copying or purchasing a composition, using ideas, paragraphs, sentences, phrases or words written by another, or using data and/or statistics compiled by another without giving appropriate citation. Another example of academic dishonesty (cheating) is the submission of the same, or essentially the same, paper or other assignment for credit in two different courses without receiving prior approval.

Consequences of Academic Dishonesty

When a faculty member discovers a violation of the university's policy of academic integrity, the faculty member is required to notify the university's Coordinator of Student Discipline and Judicial Affairs of the alleged violation, including the name(s) of the student(s) suspected, the class in which the alleged violation occurred, the circumstances of the alleged violation, and the evidence (including witnesses) supporting the allegation. The faculty member shall also formally notify the student(s) suspected of violating the university's policy of academic integrity, the department chair, and the school dean. The Coordinator for Student Discipline and Judicial Affairs shall conduct an investigation, confer with the faculty member, student(s), and any witnesses identified, and review all evidence submitted by the faculty member and student(s). Normally, the Coordinator for Student Discipline and Judicial Affairs shall make a settlement agreement with the student for his/her first violation of academic integrity with the following sanctions:

• final course grade of "F"

• one-year "academic probation" requiring a meeting with the Coordinator of Student Discipline and Judicial Affairs prior to registration for each subsequent academic term of the probationary year.

The settlement agreement for the first offense shall not be placed in the student's permanent file. If a second violation of academic integrity occurs, the student shall be suspended from CSUB for a minimum of one year. A third violation shall result in expulsion from the CSU for life. All suspensions and expulsions shall become a part of the student's permanent record. Under the Student Discipline Procedures, a student may appeal any sanction employed by the University regarding an allegation of violating the university's policy of academic integrity. The Student Discipline Officer serves under the Dean of Undergraduate Studies. The Office of Undergraduate Studies coordinates all arrangements for the appeals.

10240919R0

Made in the USA
Lexington, KY
08 July 2011